101 BIBLE ADVENTURES

101 BIBLE ADVENTURES

THE ULTIMATE QUEST FOR TRUTH!

Carolyn Larsen

Illustrated by Rick Incrocci

TYNDALE KiDS

Tyndale House Publishers, Inc.
Carol Stream, Illinois

Visit Tyndale's website for kids at www.tyndale.com/kids.

TYNDALE is a registered trademark of Tyndale House Publishers, Inc. The Tyndale Kids logo is a trademark of Tyndale House Publishers, Inc.

101 Bible Adventures: The Ultimate Quest for Truth!

Edited by Betty Free Swanberg

For manufacturing information regarding this product, please call 1-800-323-9400.

Library of Congress Cataloging-in-Publication Data

Larsen, Carolyn, date.
  101 Bible adventures : the ultimate quest for truth! / Carolyn Larsen.
      p. cm.
  ISBN 978-1-4143-4997-8 (sc)
  1. Bible stories, English. 2. Heroes in the Bible—Juvenile literature.
  I. Title.
  BS551.3.L34 2012
  220.9′505—dc23   2011042377

Printed in the United States of America

18	17	16	15	14	13	12
7	6	5	4	3	2	

Contents

Dear Parents,

Your children are gifts from God—I'm sure that isn't news to you. He has entrusted you with the responsibility of teaching them about God's love and his Word. As parents, you have the joy and the calling to live out your faith day in and day out. You can show your children that Christianity is not just for Sundays—it guides and challenges you every day of the week, in all you do.

This action-packed Bible storybook is unique because it gives background information on each Bible story, providing setting and context. Each story includes a key Bible verse, which focuses on the life lesson of the reading. The story itself is taken directly from the New Living Translation, an accurate and easy-to-understand translation of God's Word. The "Now What?" section helps kids make applications to their lives and serves as a prompt for discussion.

As your children read through this book, they will gain a better understanding of God's Word and the practicality of the Bible's teachings for daily life. Your children will gain an awareness of God's work in people's lives, whether through stressful situations or miraculous interventions. As your children see God in action in the stories, they will learn to trust him each day and bring problems, concerns, and requests to him in prayer.

In Deuteronomy 6:6-9 we see clearly that God commands parents to make Scripture a part of everyday life: "You must commit yourselves wholeheartedly to these commands that I am giving you today. Repeat them again and again to your children. Talk about them when you are at home and when you are on the road, when you are going to bed and when you are getting up. Tie them to your hands and wear them on your forehead as reminders. Write them on the doorposts of your house and on your gates."

My prayer is that this book will be a helpful tool for you as your children learn to make God's Word a daily part of their lives!

Blessings,
Carolyn Larsen

GOD MAKES A WORLD

What's Up

Before Creation, there was nothing. There was no one—except God. Everything was just dark emptiness. There were no people, no animals, no trees, and no plants. There were no oceans or continents, not even earth and sky! There was nothing. God spoke these words and started the creation of everything: "Let there be light!" His most amazing creation was the first man and woman—made to be very much like God himself.

Action Adventure from Genesis 1; 2:3

In the beginning God created the heavens and the earth. The earth was empty, and darkness covered the deep waters. God said, "Let there be light," and there was light. God called the light "day" and the darkness "night." Evening passed and morning came, marking the first day.

Then God said, "Let there be a space to separate the waters of the heavens from the waters of the earth." God called the space "sky." Evening passed and morning came, marking the second day.

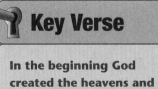

Key Verse

In the beginning God created the heavens and the earth.

Genesis 1:1

Then God said, "Let the waters beneath the sky flow together into one place, so dry ground may appear." God called the dry ground "land" and the waters "seas." Then God said, "Let the land sprout with every sort of seed-bearing plant, and trees that grow seed-bearing fruit. These seeds will then produce the kinds of plants and trees from which they came." And evening passed and morning came, marking the third day.

Then God said, "Let lights appear in the sky to separate the day from the night." God made two great lights—the larger one to govern the day, and the smaller one to govern the night. He also made the stars. And evening passed and morning came, marking the fourth day.

Then God said, "Let the waters swarm with fish and

other life. Let the skies be filled with birds of every kind." Then God blessed them, saying, "Let the fish fill the seas, and let the birds multiply on the earth." And evening passed and morning came, marking the fifth day.

Then God said, "Let the earth produce every sort of animal." God made all sorts of wild animals, livestock, and small animals, each able to produce offspring of the same kind.

Is this what God intended?

Then God said, "Let us make human beings to be like us. They will reign over the fish in the sea, the birds in the sky, the livestock, all the wild animals on the earth, and the small animals that scurry along the ground." So God created human beings in his own image; male and female he created them. [He] said, "Be fruitful and multiply."

Then God said, "I have given you every seed-bearing plant and all the fruit trees for your food." God looked over all he had made, and he saw that it was very good! And evening passed and morning came, marking the sixth day.

And God blessed the seventh day and declared it holy, because it was the day when he rested from all his work of creation.

Now What?

It's amazing to look around at the world and understand that God created everything you can see. From the tiniest bug to the mammoth killer whales—from little yellow flowers to giant redwood trees—God thought up every bit of it and made every single thing himself. God's most special creation was saved for last—the first man and woman. He made humans to be able to think and feel—like he does. You are made in God's image, to be like him. Stop right now and thank him for his wonderful creations—and for making you!

PROBLEMS IN THE GARDEN

What's Up

God gave Adam and Eve just one rule to obey. It shouldn't have been hard. After all, God gave them everything they needed to live: a beautiful garden for their home and all the food they needed. But the sneaky serpent didn't want them to obey God. He tricked Eve into breaking God's one rule. She got Adam to break the rule too. So God had to punish them.

Action Adventure from Genesis 3

The serpent was the shrewdest of all the animals God made. One day he asked the woman, "Did God really say you must not eat the fruit from any of the trees in the garden?"

"Of course we may eat from the trees in the garden," the woman replied. "It's only the fruit from the tree in the middle of the garden that we are not allowed to eat. God said, 'You must not eat it or even touch it; if you do, you will die.'"

"You won't die!" the serpent replied. "God knows that you will be like God, knowing both good and evil."

The woman was convinced. So she took some of the fruit and ate it. Then she gave some to her husband. At that moment they suddenly felt shame at their nakedness. So they sewed fig leaves together to cover themselves.

The man and his wife heard God walking in the garden. So they hid. Then God called to the man, "Where are you?"

He replied, "I hid. I was afraid because I was naked."

"Who told you that you were naked?" God asked. "Have you eaten from the tree whose fruit I commanded you not to eat?"

The man replied, "The woman gave me the fruit, and I ate it."

Key Verse

Adam's one sin brings condemnation for everyone, but Christ's one act of righteousness brings a right relationship with God and new life for everyone.

Romans 5:18

Then God asked the woman, "What have you done?"

"The serpent deceived me," she replied. "That's why I ate it."

Then God said to the serpent, "Because you have done this, you are cursed. You will crawl on your belly in the dust as long as you live."

Then he said to the woman, "In pain you will give birth."

To the man he said, "Since you ate from the tree the ground is cursed. You will struggle to scratch a living from it. By the sweat of your brow will you have food to eat until you return to the ground from which you were made. For you were made from dust, and to dust you will return."

God made clothing from animal skins for Adam and his wife [Eve].

I'm sure God would understand.

Then God said, "The human beings have become like us, knowing both good and evil." So God banished them from the Garden of Eden. God stationed mighty cherubim to the east of the Garden of Eden. And he placed a flaming sword that flashed back and forth to guard the way to the tree of life.

Now What?

Ever since the first man and woman walked on earth, people have been disobeying God. It's called sin. God must feel bad that the people he loves so much do not love him enough to obey him. Just as God punished Adam and Eve, he knew we would have to be punished for our sin too. But God loved people so much that he sent Jesus to die for our sins. That love is the main story of the whole Bible!

THE BIG FLOOD

What's Up

After Adam and Eve disobeyed God, people began doing worse things. Before long no one cared about obeying God. It broke God's heart when people would not change their ways. Finally he decided to wipe out all the people on earth and start over. Only one man obeyed God. His name was Noah. God told Noah about his plan to send a big flood to cover the earth. He wanted Noah and his family to be safe.

Action Adventure from Genesis 6:9-22; 7:1-5, 11, 17-24

Noah was the only blameless person living on earth at the time, and he walked in close fellowship with God. Noah was the father of three sons: Shem, Ham, and Japheth.

Now God saw that the earth was filled with violence. So God said to Noah, "I have decided to destroy all living creatures, for they have filled the earth with violence. Build a large boat from cypress wood and waterproof it with tar. Make the boat 450 feet long, 75 feet wide, and 45 feet high. Leave an 18-inch opening below the roof all the way around the boat. Put the door on the side, and build three decks inside the boat. I am about to cover the earth with a flood that will destroy every living thing that breathes. So enter the boat—you and your wife and your sons and their wives."

Noah did everything exactly as God had commanded him.

When everything was ready, the LORD said to Noah, "Go into the boat with all your family. Take with you seven pairs of each animal I have approved for eating and for sacrifice, and take one pair of each of the

Key Verse

The LORD is my light and my salvation—so why should I be afraid? The LORD is my fortress, protecting me from danger, so why should I tremble?

Psalm 27:1

others. There must be a male and a female in each pair to ensure that all life will survive on the earth after the flood. Seven days from now I will make the rains pour down on the earth. It will rain for forty days and forty nights, until I have wiped from the earth all the living things I have created."

Noah did everything as the LORD commanded him.

When Noah was 600 years old, all the underground waters erupted from the earth, and the rain fell from the sky. For forty days the floodwaters grew deeper, covering the ground and lifting the boat high above the earth. As the waters rose higher and higher above the ground, the boat floated safely on the surface. Finally, the water covered even the highest mountains on the earth. All the

You wanted it HOW big?

living things on earth died— birds, domestic animals, wild animals, small animals that scurry along the ground, and all the people. Everything that breathed and lived on dry land died. The only people who survived were Noah and those with him in the boat. And the floodwaters covered the earth for 150 days.

Now What?

God didn't mess around where sin was concerned. He got tired of people disobeying him and ignoring him, so he wiped out all people except Noah and his family. God still doesn't put up with sin. He will never allow it to enter heaven. However, his extreme love is at work. He sent Jesus to live, teach, die, and live again. Jesus' death paid the price for all our sins. When we believe in Jesus, confess our sin, and accept Jesus as our Savior from sin, we are free from having to pay sin's price!

A RAINBOW PROMISE

What's Up

All the people on earth died in the great Flood. The animals, plants, and trees—everything God had created—died, except the people and animals on the boat. God saved each of them. When the floodwaters were gone and it was safe, God brought the people and animals out of the boat. Then he promised he would never send a flood so big that it destroyed the whole earth again.

Action Adventure from Genesis 8:1-22; 9:12-17

God remembered Noah and all the animals with him in the boat. He sent a wind to blow across the earth, and the floodwaters began to recede. The underground waters stopped flowing, and the torrential rains from the sky were stopped. After 150 days, the boat came to rest on the mountains of Ararat.

After another forty days, Noah released a raven. The bird flew back and forth until the floodwaters on the earth had dried up. He also released a dove to see if the water had receded and it could find dry ground. But the dove could find no place to land because the water still covered the ground. So it returned to the boat. After waiting another seven days, Noah released the dove again. This time the dove returned to him with a fresh olive leaf in its beak. Then Noah knew that the floodwaters were almost gone. He waited another seven days and then released the dove again. This time it did not come back.

On the first day of the new year, ten and a half months after the flood began, the floodwaters had almost dried up. Noah lifted back the covering of the boat and saw that the surface of the ground was drying. Two more

Key Verse

When I see the rainbow in the clouds, I will remember the eternal covenant between God and every living creature on earth.

Genesis 9:16

months went by, and at last the earth was dry!

Then God said to Noah, "Leave the boat. Release the animals so they can be fruitful and multiply."

Then Noah built an altar to the LORD and sacrificed burnt offerings. The LORD was pleased with the aroma of the sacrifice and said, "I will never again destroy all living things. As long as the earth remains, there will be planting and harvest, cold and heat, summer and winter, day and night."

Then God said, "I have placed my rainbow in the clouds. It is the sign of my covenant with you and with all the earth. When I send clouds over the earth, the rainbow will appear in the clouds, and I will remember my covenant with you and with all

WHEW! I was worried this time. God still does love me!

living creatures. Never again will the floodwaters destroy all life. When I see the rainbow in the clouds, I will remember the eternal covenant between God and every living creature on earth." Then God said to Noah, "Yes, this rainbow is the sign of the covenant I am confirming with all the creatures on earth."

Now What?

Sometimes when parents discipline their children, they say, "This hurts me more than it hurts you." It's true—it's not fun to discipline someone you love. God didn't like the fact that human beings chose to become disobedient and evil. When they made that choice, he couldn't put up with it. He had to do something, even though it may have been painful. But God promised Noah he would never do anything so drastic again. Every time you see a rainbow, you can remember that God loves *you*! What a beautiful reminder of his love and his promise!

THE TOWER OF TROUBLE

What's Up

At one time everyone on earth spoke the same language. Then some people decided to build a tower that would reach all the way to heaven. They thought the tower would make them famous. God was not happy about their plan. He knew they would start thinking they were smarter and more important than him. So God made them all speak different languages. Then they could no longer understand each other and try to act more important than God by building the tower.

Action Adventure from Genesis 11:1-9

At one time all the people of the world spoke the same language and used the same words. As the people migrated to the east, they found a plain in the land of Babylonia and settled there.

They began saying to each other, "Let's make bricks and harden them with fire." (In this region bricks were used instead of stone, and tar was used for mortar.) Then they said, "Come, let's build a great city for ourselves with a tower that reaches into the sky. This will make us famous and keep us from being scattered all over the world."

But the LORD came down to look at the city and the tower the people were building. "Look!" he said. "The people are united, and they all speak the same language. After this, nothing they set out to do will be impossible for them! Come, let's go down and confuse the people with different languages. Then they won't be able to understand each other."

Key Verse

You must worship no other gods, for the LORD, whose very name is Jealous, is a God who is jealous about his relationship with you.

Exodus 34:14

In that way, the LORD scattered them all over the world, and they stopped building the city. That is why the city was called Babel, because that is where the LORD confused the people with different languages. In this way he scattered them all over the world.

No. No. No. I said BRICKS! Can't you understand me?

Now What?

God loves his people. He wants to take care of his children and guide them—just like he promised to do. When people try to push God out of the way, he will work hard to get their attention and focus them back on how much he loves them—just as he did with the builders of this big tower. What competes with your love for God? How does he try to get your attention and love focused back on him? And how do you respond to him?

ABRAM'S BIG ADVENTURE

What's Up

God told Abram to leave his hometown. He didn't tell Abram where he was sending him, but Abram obeyed. God promised to bless him and to keep him safe. However, Abram didn't trust God. He lied to the Egyptians and said that Sarai was his sister instead of his wife. The Egyptian king took Sarai to his palace. He planned for her to become one of his wives, and God punished the king for that.

Action Adventure from Genesis 12:1-20

The LORD said to Abram, "Leave your country and go to the land that I will show you. I will make you into a great nation. I will bless you and make you famous, and you will be a blessing to others. I will bless those who bless you and curse those who treat you with contempt. All the families on earth will be blessed through you."

So Abram departed as the LORD instructed. Abram was seventy-five years old when he left Haran. He took his wife, Sarai, his nephew Lot, and all his wealth—his livestock and all the people he had taken into his household—and headed for the land of Canaan. When they arrived in Canaan, Abram traveled through the land as far as Shechem. There he set up camp beside the oak of Moreh. At that time, the area was inhabited by Canaanites.

Then the LORD appeared to Abram and said, "I will give this land to your descendants." And Abram built an altar there and dedicated it to the LORD. After that, Abram traveled south and set up camp in the hill country. There he built another altar and he worshiped the LORD. Then Abram continued traveling south by stages toward the Negev.

Key Verse

Trust in the LORD with all your heart; do not depend on your own understanding. Seek his will in all you do, and he will show you which path to take.

Proverbs 3:5-6

At that time a severe famine struck the land of Canaan, forcing Abram to go down to Egypt, where he lived as a foreigner. As he was approaching the border of Egypt, Abram said to his wife, Sarai, "You are a very beautiful woman. When the Egyptians see you, they will say, 'This is his wife. Let's kill him; then we can have her!' So please tell them you are my sister. Then they will spare my life and treat me well because of their interest in you."

And sure enough, when Abram arrived in Egypt, everyone noticed Sarai's beauty. When the palace officials saw her, they sang her praises to Pharaoh, and Sarai was taken into his palace. Then Pharaoh gave Abram many gifts because of her—sheep, goats, cattle, male and female donkeys, male and female servants, and camels.

I don't know if we're almost there. I don't even know where we're going.

But the LORD sent plagues upon Pharaoh and his household. "[Abram,] why didn't you tell me she was your wife? Why did you say, 'She is my sister,' and allow me to take her as my wife? Take her and get out of here!" Pharaoh ordered, and he sent Abram out of the country, along with his wife and all his possessions.

Now What?

The problem with Abram in this story is that he didn't really trust God. If he had really trusted God to keep him safe, he would have told the truth about Sarai being his wife. He would have believed that God could and would keep him safe, no matter what. Trusting God is more than just saying that you trust him. It's believing everything he says in his Word with all your heart and knowing that he will take care of you even in situations that seem pretty scary. Trusting God completely lets you relax and feel calm because you know he will take care of everything.

ABRAM TO THE RESCUE!

What's Up

Kings of several nations banded together to rebel against King Kedorlaomer (kay-dor-lay-OH-mer). They were tired of being ruled by him. When Sodom and Gomorrah were captured, Abram's nephew Lot was taken captive. But Abram couldn't let the enemy army keep his nephew. He raced to Lot's rescue!

Action Adventure from Genesis 14:1-16

[War broke out near where Abram and Lot were living. The kings of Babylonia, Ellasar, Elam, and Goiim fought against the kings of Sodom, Gomorrah, Admah, Zeboiim, and Bela. This second group of kings joined together to fight. For twelve years they had been under King Kedorlaomer's rule, but in the thirteenth year they fought back against him.]

One year later Kedorlaomer and his allies arrived and defeated the Rephaites, the Zuzites, the Emites, and the Horites. Then they turned back and conquered all the territory of the Amalekites, and also the Amorites living in Hazazon-tamar.

Then the rebel kings of Sodom, Gomorrah, Admah, Zeboiim, and Bela (also called Zoar) prepared for battle in the valley of the Dead Sea. They fought against King Kedorlaomer of Elam, King Tidal of Goiim, King Amraphel of Babylonia, and King Arioch of Ellasar—four kings against five. As it happened, the valley of the Dead Sea was filled with tar pits. And as the army of the kings of Sodom and Gomorrah fled, some fell into the tar pits, while the rest escaped into the mountains. The victorious invaders then plundered Sodom and Gomorrah, and headed

Key Verse

Show me your unfailing love in wonderful ways. By your mighty power you rescue those who seek refuge from their enemies.

Psalm 17:7

for home, taking with them all the spoils of war and the food supplies. They also captured Lot—Abram's nephew who lived in Sodom—and carried off everything he owned.

But one of Lot's men escaped and reported everything to Abram the Hebrew, who was living near the oak grove belonging to Mamre the Amorite. Mamre and his relatives were Abram's allies. When Abram heard that his nephew Lot had been captured, he [and] 318 trained men who had been born into his household pursued Kedorlaomer's army. He caught up with them at Dan. There he divided his men and attacked during the night. Kedorlaomer's

Thanks, Uncle Abe. That was too close for comfort!

army fled, but Abram chased them as far as Hobah, north of Damascus. Abram recovered all the goods that had been taken, and he brought back his nephew Lot with his possessions and all the women and other captives.

Now What?

Abram took care of his family. When he heard that his nephew Lot was in trouble, he organized a rescue team. Abram knew that God would strengthen him and fight for him as he went to rescue Lot, so Abram was not afraid. God will always fight for you, too. So, even when life seems scary, don't be afraid. Just trust God. And when you see a friend or family member who is in trouble, remember to ask God to help you do whatever you can to help with the rescue!

GAME OVER

What's Up

To solve the fights between Abram's workers and Lot's workers, Lot had moved to a town called Sodom. However, Sodom was filled with wicked people doing evil things. God waited for the people to change their ways, but they would not do it. So God decided to destroy the town. Abram asked him to save Lot, but Lot had to listen to God's messengers!

Action Adventure from Genesis 19:1-3, 12-26

That evening two angels came to the city of Sodom. Lot welcomed them and bowed with his face to the ground. "My lords," he said, "come to my home and be my guests for the night. You may then get up early in the morning and be on your way again."

"Oh no," they replied. "We'll just spend the night out here in the city square."

But Lot insisted, so at last they went home with him. Lot prepared a feast for them, and they ate. Meanwhile, the angels questioned Lot. "Do you have any other relatives here in the city?" they asked. "Get them out of this place—your sons-in-law, sons, daughters, or anyone else. For we are about to destroy this city completely. The outcry against this place is so great it has reached the LORD, and he has sent us to destroy it." So Lot rushed out to tell his daughters' fiancés, "Quick, get out of the city! The LORD is about to destroy it." But the young men thought he was only joking.

At dawn the next morning the angels became insistent. "Hurry," they said to Lot. "Take your wife and your two daughters. Get out right now, or you will be swept away!"

Key Verse

The LORD leads with unfailing love and faithfulness all who keep his covenant and obey his demands.

Psalm 25:10

The angels seized [Lot's] hand and the hands of his wife and two daughters and rushed them to safety outside the city. One of the angels ordered, "Run for your lives! And don't look back or stop anywhere in the valley! Escape to the mountains, or you will be swept away!"

"Oh no, my lord!" Lot begged. "You have been so gracious to me, but I cannot go to the mountains. There is a small village nearby. Please let me go there instead. Then my life will be saved."

"All right," the angel said, "I will grant your request. But hurry!" Lot reached the village just as the sun was rising over the horizon. Then the LORD rained down fire and burning

Keep going. I would hate to think what could happen if you looked back.

sulfur from the sky on Sodom and Gomorrah. He destroyed them, wiping out all the people and every bit of vegetation. But Lot's wife looked back as she was following behind him, and she turned into a pillar of salt.

Now What?

God won't put up with sin and wickedness. He has made that very clear all through his Word, the Bible. If the people of Sodom had listened and obeyed, things would have been different for them. God protected Lot because he obeyed. It's easy to trust God when things are going great. It's easy to obey when he asks something easy. But when God asks you to do something that looks hard, that's when it is most important to obey. So ask God what he wants you to do. Read his Word so you know how he wants you to live. Then do it!

A TEST FOR ABRAHAM

What's Up

God asked Abraham, whose name used to be Abram, to do something really hard. God asked him to give his precious son, Isaac, as a sacrifice— an offering to God. Abraham loved Isaac. But he loved God more. And his faith was so strong that he believed if Isaac died, God could bring him back to life. (That's what Hebrews 11:19 says.) God was testing Abraham to see just how much Abraham loved him. So, even though it had to have been the hardest thing he had ever done, Abraham raised a knife over his son. That's when he heard God call, "Wait!"

Action Adventure from Genesis 22:1-18

God tested Abraham's faith. "Abraham!" God called.

"Yes," he replied. "Here I am."

"Take your only son, Isaac, whom you love so much, and sacrifice him as a burnt offering on one of the mountains, which I will show you." The next morning Abraham got up early. He took two of his servants, along with his son, Isaac. Then he chopped wood for a fire for a burnt offering and set out for the place God told him about. On the third day of their journey, Abraham saw the place in the distance. "Stay here with the donkey," Abraham told the servants. "The boy and I will worship there, and then we will come back."

Abraham placed the wood for the burnt offering on Isaac's shoulders, while he carried the fire and the knife. As the two of them walked, Isaac said, "Father?"

"Yes, my son?" Abraham replied.

"We have the fire and the wood," the boy said, "but where is the sheep for the burnt offering?"

"God will provide a sheep, my son," Abraham answered. And they walked on together.

Key Verse

Now I know that you truly fear God. You have not withheld from me even your son, your only son.

Genesis 22:12

When they arrived at the place God had told him to go, Abraham built an altar and arranged the wood on it. Then he tied his son, Isaac, and laid him on the altar on top of the wood. And Abraham picked up the knife to kill his son as a sacrifice. At that moment the angel of the LORD called to him from heaven, "Abraham! Abraham!"

"Yes," Abraham replied. "Here I am!"

"Don't lay a hand on the boy!" the angel said. "Do not hurt him in any way, for now I know that you truly fear God. You have not withheld from me your only son."

Abraham looked up and saw a ram caught by its horns. So he took the ram and sacrificed it in place of his son. Abraham named the place Yahweh-Yireh (which means "the LORD will provide").

Then the angel of the LORD called again to Abraham. "The LORD says because you have not withheld your only son, I swear by my own name that I will bless you. I will multiply your descendants beyond number, like the stars in the sky and the sand on the seashore. Your descendants will conquer the cities of their enemies. And through your descendants all the nations of the earth will be blessed—all because you have obeyed me."

That was just a little too close.

Now What?

There's one thing God cares about the most, and that's how much you love him. God wanted to know that Abraham loved him more than anything in the world—even more than his son. Is there anything in your life that is more important to you than God? A family member? A friend? A hobby? A dream for the future? Give it to God. Trust him and love him more than anything else. You won't be sorry!

QUARRELS AND QUESTIONS

What's Up

When Isaac grew up and married Rebekah, he lied about Rebekah being his wife. He was afraid that people might hurt him so they could get her. (Does that sound like what Isaac's father did in Egypt many years earlier in "Abram's Big Adventure"?) Isaac finally had to tell the truth about Rebekah. After that, God blessed him with good crops. Isaac was a foreigner in the land where he lived—a stranger who had moved there from somewhere far away. Over and over again, the king saw that God was with Isaac. That frightened him, so he asked Isaac to leave.

Action Adventure from Genesis 26:1-30

A famine struck the land, so Isaac moved to Gerar, where Abimelech, king of the Philistines, lived. The LORD appeared to Isaac and said, "Live as a foreigner in this land and I will bless you."

So Isaac stayed in Gerar. When the men there asked about his wife, Rebekah, he said, "She is my sister." He was afraid to say, "She is my wife." He thought, "They will kill me to get her, because she is so beautiful." Later, Abimelech saw Isaac caressing Rebekah. Immediately, Abimelech called for Isaac and exclaimed, "She is your wife! Why did you say, 'She is my sister'?"

"I was afraid someone would kill me to get her," Isaac replied.

"One of my people might have taken your wife, and you would have made us guilty of great sin," Abimelech said. Then Abimelech issued a proclamation: "Anyone who touches this man or his wife will be put to death!"

When Isaac planted his crops that year, he harvested a hundred times more grain than he planted, for the LORD blessed

Key Verse

What does the LORD your God require of you? He requires only that you fear the LORD your God, and live in a way that pleases him, and love him and serve him with all your heart and soul.

Deuteronomy 10:12

him. He acquired so many flocks of sheep and goats, herds of cattle, and servants that the Philistines became jealous of him. So [they] filled up Isaac's wells with dirt.

Finally, Abimelech ordered Isaac to leave. "Go somewhere else," he said, "for you have become too powerful for us." So Isaac moved to the Gerar Valley. He reopened the wells his father had dug, which the Philistines had filled in after Abraham's death.

Isaac's servants discovered a well of fresh water. But the shepherds from Gerar claimed, "This is our water." They argued with Isaac's herdsmen. Isaac's men then dug another well, but again there was a dispute over it. Isaac moved on and dug another well. This time there was no dispute over it.

From there Isaac moved to Beersheba, where the LORD appeared to him. "Do not be afraid, for I am with you and

Wow! I guess honesty really does pay.

will bless you," [God said]. Isaac built an altar there and worshiped the LORD.

One day King Abimelech came from Gerar. [He said,] "We can see that the LORD is with you. So we want to enter into a sworn treaty with you. Swear that you will not harm us. We have always treated you well, and we sent you away in peace. And look how the LORD has blessed you!" So Isaac prepared a feast to celebrate the treaty.

Now What?

Once Isaac began obeying God, he was blessed beyond anything he could imagine. God protected him. And God provided for him, giving him everything he needed. All of this happened while Isaac lived as a foreigner in a land where people did not believe in God. Obeying God brings good things. Sometimes the blessings of obedience do not come right away. But if you trust God's promises, you know they will come. So . . . start celebrating!

FOOLING A FATHER

What's Up

There were many honors and blessings given to the oldest sons in Hebrew families. Isaac and Rebekah had twin sons, Esau and Jacob. Even though the boys were twins, Esau was the firstborn because he was born a few minutes before Jacob. Esau didn't care about his rights as the firstborn son though. He gave them away easily. Then Rebekah helped Jacob plan a way to steal the blessing that also should have been Esau's. No good could come of this.

Action Adventure from Genesis 25:20-33; 27:1-35, 40-44

Isaac married Rebekah, and [she] became pregnant with twins. When the time came to give birth, the first one was very red. So they named him Esau. The other twin was born grasping Esau's heel. So they named him Jacob.

One day Jacob was cooking stew. Esau said, "Give me some!"

Jacob replied, "Trade me your rights as the firstborn son."

"I'm dying of starvation!" said Esau. "What good is my birthright?" So Esau swore an oath, selling his rights as the firstborn to his brother, Jacob.

When Isaac was old and turning blind, he called Esau and said, "Hunt wild game for me to eat. Then I will pronounce the blessing that belongs to you, my firstborn son."

When Esau left to hunt, [Rebekah] said to her son Jacob, "Bring me two goats. I'll prepare your father's favorite dish. He can eat it and bless you."

Jacob replied, "Esau is hairy, and my skin is smooth. What if my father touches me? He'll see that I'm trying to trick him."

[Rebekah] replied, "Let the curse fall on me!"

So Jacob got the goats. Rebekah prepared a meal. She took Esau's clothes and gave them to Jacob. She covered his

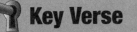

Key Verse

Greed causes fighting; trusting the LORD leads to prosperity.

Proverbs 28:25

arms and neck with the skin of the goats.

Jacob took the food to his father. [Isaac asked,] "Who are you—Esau or Jacob?"

Jacob replied, "It's Esau. Here is the wild game. Eat it so you can give me your blessing."

Isaac said, "Come closer so I can touch you and make sure you really are Esau." Isaac touched him. "The voice is Jacob's, but the hands are Esau's. Let me eat, and I will give you my blessing." So Isaac ate and he blessed his son.

Esau returned, prepared a meal, and brought it to his father. "Sit up and eat so you can give me your blessing," he said.

But Isaac asked, "Who are you?"

Esau replied, "It's your firstborn son, Esau."

Isaac said, "Then who just served me? I have already eaten, and I blessed him before you came. That blessing must stand!"

I can't believe you fell for that!

"Bless me, too!" [Esau] begged.

Isaac said, "Your brother tricked me. He has taken your blessing. You will serve your brother."

Esau hated Jacob. "I will kill my brother, Jacob."

Rebekah heard about Esau's plans and told [Jacob], "Flee to my brother, Laban, in Haran. Stay there until your brother cools off."

Now What?

There are many wrong things about this story— from Esau not caring about his birthright and giving it away, to Rebekah helping Jacob steal his brother's blessing, to Jacob tricking his father. The bottom line is greed— wanting more than you should have. Rebekah wanted Jacob to have something that didn't really belong to him, and he was willing to go along with that. Greed will always get you in trouble. It leads to lies and tricks and sometimes even hurting people. Is greed something you struggle with? Pray now and ask God to help you let it go!

12

ANGELS ALL AROUND

What's Up

Jacob tricked his father and cheated his brother. Then he had to run for his life to escape his brother's anger. But God still had a plan for Jacob. God let Jacob know he was with Jacob by sending him a beautiful dream. It was a dream about angels, with a simple promise that God would stay with Jacob.

Action Adventure from Genesis 28:10-22

Jacob left Beersheba and traveled toward Haran. At sundown he arrived at a good place to set up camp and stopped there for the night. Jacob found a stone to rest his head against and lay down to sleep. As he slept, he dreamed of a stairway that reached from the earth up to heaven. And he saw the angels of God going up and down the stairway.

At the top of the stairway stood the LORD, and he said, "I am the LORD, the God of your grandfather Abraham, and the God of your father, Isaac. The ground you are lying on belongs to you. I am giving it to you and your descendants. Your descendants will be as numerous as the dust of the earth! They will spread out in all directions—to the west and the east, to the north and the south. And all the families of the earth will be blessed through you and your descendants. What's more, I am with you, and I will protect you wherever you go. One day I will bring you back to this land. I will not leave you until I have finished giving you everything I have promised you."

🔑 Key Verse

At the top of the stairway stood the LORD, and he said, "I am the LORD, the God of your grandfather Abraham, and the God of your father, Isaac. The ground you are lying on belongs to you. I am giving it to you and your descendants."

Genesis 28:13

Then Jacob awoke from his sleep and said, "Surely the LORD is in this place, and I wasn't even aware of it!" But he was also afraid and said, "What an awesome place this is! It is none other than the house of God, the very gateway to heaven!"

The next morning Jacob got up very early. He took the stone he had rested his head against, and he set it upright as a memorial pillar. Then he poured olive oil over it. He named that place Bethel (which means "house of God").

Then Jacob made this vow: "If God will be with me and protect me on this journey, and if he will provide me with food and clothing, and if I return

I better get going. It sounds like I'm going to be busy!

safely to my father's home, then the LORD will certainly be my God. And this memorial pillar I have set up will become a place for worshiping God, and I will present to God a tenth of everything he gives me."

Now What?

Do you ever wonder if God will turn away from you if you behave badly? Do you think he might give up on you if you do something wrong? Then the story of Jacob should make you feel good. Jacob did some pretty mean things—cheating his brother and tricking his father—but God still sent angels to Jacob's dreams. He still promised to bless Jacob more than Jacob ever could have dreamed. God has good plans for every person's life, and he will see those plans through to the end. Why not stop right now and thank God for his love, his forgiveness, and his wonderful plans for you?

COMING HOME

What's Up

Life turned out pretty good for Jacob. God gave him a big family and helped him become very rich. But when Jacob heard that his brother, Esau, was close by, he was afraid. Esau had good reason to be mad at his brother. Jacob had cheated Esau and tricked their father into giving him Esau's blessing. So, what would Esau do when he saw his brother again after many years?

Action Adventure from Genesis 33

Jacob saw Esau coming with his 400 men. So he divided the children among Leah, Rachel, and his two servant wives. He put the servant wives and their children at the front, Leah and her children next, and Rachel and Joseph last. Then Jacob went on ahead. As he approached his brother, he bowed to the ground seven times before him. Then Esau ran to meet him and threw his arms around his neck, and kissed him. And they both wept.

Then Esau looked at the women and children and asked, "Who are these people with you?"

"These are the children God has given to me," Jacob replied. Then the servant wives came forward with their children and bowed before him. Next came Leah with her children, and they bowed before him. Finally, Joseph and Rachel came forward and bowed before him.

"And what were all the flocks and herds I met as I came?" Esau asked.

Jacob replied, "They are a gift, my lord, to ensure your friendship."

"My brother, I have plenty," Esau answered. "Keep what you have for yourself."

🔑 Key Verse

Even if that person wrongs you seven times a day and each time turns again and asks forgiveness, you must forgive.

Luke 17:4

But Jacob insisted, "No, if I have found favor with you, please accept this gift from me. And what a relief to see your friendly smile. It is like seeing the face of God! Please take this gift I have brought you, for I have more than enough." Esau finally accepted the gift.

"Well," Esau said, "let's be going. I will lead the way."

But Jacob replied, "You can see, my lord, that some of the children are very young, and the flocks and herds have their young, too. If they are driven too hard, even for one day, all the animals could die. Please go ahead. We will follow slowly, at a pace that is comfortable for the livestock and the children. I will meet you at Seir."

"All right," Esau said, "but at least let some of my men guide and protect you."

Jacob responded, "That's

Whew! I wasn't sure how that was going to turn out.

not necessary. It's enough that you've received me warmly, my lord!"

So Esau turned around and started back to Seir that same day. Jacob, on the other hand, traveled on to the town of Shechem, in the land of Canaan. There he set up camp outside the town. Jacob bought the plot of land where he camped, and he built an altar.

Now What?

Esau could have been very angry at his brother, but he wasn't. Instead of holding a grudge—feeling bitter and upset—for many years, he had forgiven Jacob. Forgiveness is a wonderful thing. Have you ever needed to ask a friend for forgiveness? Did your friend forgive you? Have you ever been able to forgive someone else? It feels good to be forgiven and to forgive others. It's also important to ask God for forgiveness for your sins. Do you do that? Are there some things you need to ask him to forgive right now?

FAMILY FEUD

What's Up

Jacob had 12 sons, but his son Joseph was his favorite. It's easy to understand why Jacob's other sons were jealous of their little brother. Why should he be more special than they were? When he told his brothers about dreams he had in which they bowed down to him, Joseph's brothers got even more jealous. They decided to get rid of him. Their plan started a new chapter in Joseph's life.

Action Adventure from Genesis 37:3-36

Jacob loved Joseph more than his other children because Joseph had been born to him in his old age. Jacob had a special gift made for Joseph—a beautiful robe. His brothers hated Joseph because their father loved him more than the rest of them.

One night Joseph had a dream. "Listen to this dream," he said. "We were tying up bundles of grain. Suddenly your bundles all bowed low before mine!"

His brothers responded, "So you think you will be our king, do you?" And they hated him all the more.

Joseph had another dream and again told his brothers about it. "The sun, moon, and eleven stars bowed low before me!"

This time he told the dream to his father, but his father scolded him. "Will your mother and I and your brothers come and bow before you?" His father wondered what the dreams meant.

Joseph's brothers went to pasture their father's flocks at Shechem. When they had been gone for some time, Jacob said to Joseph, "Go and see your brothers. Bring me a report."

When Joseph's brothers saw him coming, they made plans to kill him. "Here comes the dreamer!" they said. "Let's kill him and throw him into one of these

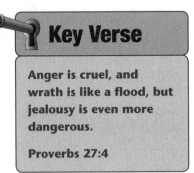

🔑 Key Verse

Anger is cruel, and wrath is like a flood, but jealousy is even more dangerous.

Proverbs 27:4

cisterns. We can tell our father, 'A wild animal has eaten him.'"

Reuben came to Joseph's rescue. "Let's not kill him," he said. "Let's just throw him into this empty cistern. Then he'll die without our laying a hand on him." Reuben was secretly planning to rescue Joseph and return him to his father.

When Joseph arrived, his brothers ripped off the beautiful robe and threw him into the cistern. The cistern was empty; there was no water in it. Then they saw a caravan of camels coming toward them. It was a group of Ishmaelite traders taking a load of gum, balm, and aromatic resin to Egypt.

Judah said, "What will we gain by killing our brother? Instead, let's sell him to those traders." His brothers agreed, and the traders took him to Egypt.

The brothers killed a young goat and dipped Joseph's robe

I think we solved that problem!

in its blood. They sent the robe to their father with this message: "Look at what we found. Doesn't this robe belong to your son?"

"Yes," he said, "it is my son's robe. A wild animal must have eaten him." He mourned deeply for his son for a long time. He refused to be comforted.

Meanwhile, the traders sold Joseph to Potiphar, an officer of Pharaoh, the king of Egypt.

Now What?

Have you ever been jealous of the good things that happened to someone else? Jealousy is hard to shut down. It can take over your thoughts and actions and make you do things that you never would have dreamed of doing. Jealousy is a terrible thing—just look at what it made Joseph's brothers do to him! But also notice how God took care of Joseph. He had plans for Joseph, and not even Joseph's brothers could ruin those plans. In fact, God used their actions to make his plans happen!

PUNISHED!

What's Up

Life seemed to go from bad to good to worse to better for Joseph. His brothers sold him into slavery, but he was such a good slave that he was put in charge of his master's house. Then he was blamed for something he didn't do, and he ended up in jail. But, once again, God was with Joseph, and he was given a responsible job in the prison.

Action Adventure from Genesis 39

When Joseph was taken to Egypt, he was purchased by Potiphar, captain of the guard for Pharaoh, the king of Egypt.

The LORD was with Joseph, so he succeeded in everything he did. Potiphar realized that the LORD was with Joseph, so he put him in charge of everything he owned. From the day Joseph was put in charge, the LORD began to bless Potiphar's household for Joseph's sake. So Potiphar gave Joseph complete responsibility over everything he owned. With Joseph there, he didn't worry about a thing.

Joseph was a very handsome young man, and Potiphar's wife soon began to look at him. "Come and sleep with me," she demanded.

"Look," he told her, "my master trusts me with everything in his household. He has held back nothing from me except you, because you are his wife. How could I do such a wicked thing? It would be a great sin against God."

She kept putting pressure on Joseph day after day, but he kept out of her way as much as possible. One day, however, no one else was around when he went in to do his work. She grabbed him by his cloak, demanding, "Sleep with me!" Joseph tore himself away, but he left his cloak in her hand as he ran from the house.

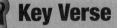
Key Verse

The LORD was with Joseph in the prison and showed him his faithful love.

Genesis 39:21

When she saw that she was holding his cloak, she called out to her servants. Soon all the men came running. "Look!" she said. "My husband has brought this Hebrew slave here to make fools of us! He came into my room, but I screamed. When he heard me scream, he ran away, but he left his cloak behind with me."

She kept the cloak until her husband came home. Then she told him her story. "That slave tried to come in and fool around with me," she said. "But when I screamed, he ran, leaving his cloak with me!"

Potiphar was furious when he heard his wife's story. So he took Joseph and threw him into the prison. But the LORD was with Joseph in the prison and showed him his faithful love.

I feel like I have been through this before!

Before long, the warden put Joseph in charge of all the other prisoners and over everything that happened in the prison. The warden had no more worries, because Joseph took care of everything. The LORD was with him and caused everything he did to succeed.

Now What?

Sometimes it's hard to see God's love in your life when things aren't going well. Trusting God's love means truly living by faith. It means believing that even when life is tough, God is still paying attention and working out his plans. Joseph's life is a perfect example of this. Even when bad things happened to Joseph, God continued to work out his plans for Joseph and to bless him in all he did. Thank God right now for his plans for you—even for the times when life is hard.

THE DREAM TELLER

What's Up

Joseph ended up in prison. Yes, he was in charge of all the other prisoners, but he was still a prisoner. However, God never left him and never stopped helping him. When a couple of prisoners had dreams, God helped Joseph explain what they meant. Then, when one of those prisoners, Pharaoh's cupbearer, was set free, he told Pharaoh about Joseph's skills. Pharaoh called Joseph to explain what his dreams meant. That was just the next step in God's plans for Joseph.

Action Adventure from Genesis 41:1-17, 24-40, 47-48, 54-57

Two years later, Pharaoh dreamed that he was standing on the bank of the Nile River. He saw seven fat cows come out of the river. Then he saw seven more cows, but these were thin. Then the thin cows ate the fat cows!

He had a second dream. This time he saw seven heads of grain, plump and beautiful, growing on a single stalk. Seven more heads of grain appeared, but these were withered by the east wind. These thin heads swallowed up the plump heads!

Pharaoh called for the wise men of Egypt. When Pharaoh told them his dreams, not one of them could tell what they meant. Finally, the king's cup-bearer spoke up. "Some time ago, you imprisoned [the chief baker and me]. One night [we] each had a dream. There was a young Hebrew man in the prison. We told him our dreams, and he told us what they meant. Everything happened just as he predicted."

Pharaoh sent for Joseph at once. Pharaoh said, "I had a dream, and no one here can tell me what it means. I have heard that you can interpret it."

Key Verse

"I know the plans I have for you," says the Lord. "They are plans for good and not for disaster, to give you a future and a hope."

Jeremiah 29:11

"It is beyond my power," Joseph replied. "But God can tell you what it means."

So Pharaoh told Joseph his dreams.

Joseph responded, "Both dreams mean the same thing. The seven healthy cows and heads of grain represent seven years of prosperity. The seven thin cows and heads of grain represent seven years of famine.

"The next seven years will be a period of prosperity throughout Egypt. Afterward there will be seven years of famine so great that it will destroy the land. Pharaoh should find a wise man and put him in charge of the land. Then Pharaoh should appoint supervisors [to] collect crops during the seven good years. Store it away [for] when the seven years of famine come."

Pharaoh said to Joseph, "No

Thank you, God.

one is as wise as you are. You will be in charge of my court, and my people will take orders from you. Only I will have a rank higher than yours."

For seven years the land produced bumper crops. During those years, Joseph stored grain. Then seven years of famine began. People from all around came to buy grain from Joseph.

Now What?

Timing is everything, and God is in charge of timing. He had plans for Joseph and worked everything out so that Joseph could do the job God had for him to do. God put Joseph just where he needed him to be for the next step in his plans for Joseph. God has plans for you, too. Thank him for his timing in your life so that he can teach you what he wants you to know and use you to do his work in the world!

17

FAMILY FORGIVENESS

What's Up

Joseph's older brothers knew that their father loved Joseph more than the rest of them. They had sold him into slavery because they were jealous of him. However, God used every bad thing that happened in Joseph's life for good until finally Joseph became the second-in-command ruler in Egypt. Then, when a famine spread across many different countries and there was nothing to eat, Joseph's brothers had to come to him to buy food. That's when everyone could see Joseph's true character.

Action Adventure from Genesis 42:1-3, 8-24; 45:1-11

When Jacob heard that grain was available in Egypt, he said to his sons, "Go and buy enough grain to keep us alive. Otherwise we'll die." So Joseph's ten older brothers went to Egypt to buy grain.

Although Joseph recognized his brothers, they didn't recognize him. He said to them, "You are spies!"

"No!" they exclaimed. "Your servants have simply come to buy food. We are all brothers. Our youngest brother is back with our father right now, and one of our brothers is no longer with us."

[Joseph said,] "This is how I will test your story. One of you must go and get your brother. I'll keep the rest of you here in prison. If it turns out that you don't have a younger brother, then I'll know you are spies."

Joseph put them in prison for three days. On the third day Joseph said to them, "Choose one of your brothers to remain in prison. The rest of you may go home with grain for your starving

> ### Key Verse
>
> Don't be upset, and don't be angry with yourselves for selling me to this place. It was God who sent me here ahead of you to preserve your lives.
>
> Genesis 45:5

families. But you must bring your youngest brother back to me. This will prove that you are telling the truth, and you will not die." They agreed.

Speaking among themselves, they said, "We are being punished because of what we did to Joseph long ago."

They didn't know that Joseph understood them, for he had been speaking to them through an interpreter. [Joseph] chose Simeon and had him tied up.

Wow! The kid sure landed on his feet!

[The other brothers went back home. Sometime later they returned to Egypt with their youngest brother, Benjamin. Joseph released Simeon and served them all a meal. Then Joseph had his silver cup placed in Benjamin's sack of grain. When it was found, he said Benjamin would be his slave. But Judah asked Joseph to let him stay instead. He did not want his father to lose another young son.]

Joseph could stand it no longer. "I am Joseph, your brother, whom you sold into slavery. It was God who sent me here ahead of you to keep you and your families alive. So it was God who sent me here, not you! Now hurry back to my father and tell him, 'This is what your son Joseph says: God has made me master over all the land of Egypt. So come down to me immediately! You can live in the region of Goshen, where you can be near me. I will take care of you there.'"

Now What?

Joseph could have used his brothers' need for food as a chance to get even with them. But Joseph wanted to serve God and obey him. So Joseph not only forgave his brothers, but he also moved them to Egypt so he could take care of them. Forgiveness is not always easy, but it's always the right thing to do. Is there someone you need to forgive? Ask God to help you with that.

A FIGHT TO SURVIVE

What's Up

God's people, the Israelites, who also came to be called the Hebrews, were safe in Egypt for a long time. Pharaoh and his people were thankful for all Joseph did to keep them safe during the famine. But when a new king came into power, Joseph's work was forgotten. The new king was afraid that the Hebrew nation was getting too big and could fight against the Egyptians. So he ordered all Hebrew baby boys to be killed at birth. God had other plans though.

Action Adventure from Exodus 1:8-10, 15-17; 2:1-10

A new king came to power in Egypt who knew nothing about Joseph or what he had done. He said to his people, "Look, the people of Israel now outnumber us and are stronger than we are. We must make a plan to keep them from growing even more. If we don't, and if war breaks out, they will join our enemies and fight against us. Then they will escape from the country."

Pharaoh, the king of Egypt, gave this order to the Hebrew midwives: "When you help the Hebrew women as they give birth, watch as they deliver. If the baby is a boy, kill him; if it is a girl, let her live." But because the midwives feared God, they refused to obey the king's orders. They allowed the boys to live, too.

About this time, a man and woman from the tribe of Levi got married. The woman became pregnant and gave birth to a son. She saw that he was a special baby and kept him hidden for three months. But when she could no longer hide him, she got a basket made of papyrus

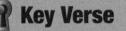

Key Verse

The Lord is my rock, my fortress, and my savior; my God is my rock, in whom I find protection. He is my shield, the power that saves me, and my place of safety.

Psalm 18:2

reeds and waterproofed it with tar and pitch. She put the baby in the basket and laid it among the reeds along the bank of the Nile River. The baby's sister then stood at a distance, watching to see what would happen to him.

Soon Pharaoh's daughter came down to bathe in the river, and her attendants walked along the riverbank. When the princess saw the basket among the reeds, she sent her maid to get it for her. When the princess opened it, she saw the baby. The little boy was crying, and she felt sorry for him. "This must be one of the Hebrew children," she said.

Then the baby's sister approached the princess. "Should I go and find one of the Hebrew women to nurse the baby for you?" she asked.

"Yes, do!" the princess replied. So the girl went and called the baby's mother.

I love it when a plan comes together!

"Take this baby and nurse him for me," the princess told the baby's mother. "I will pay you for your help." So the woman took her baby home and nursed him.

Later, when the boy was older, his mother brought him back to Pharaoh's daughter, who adopted him as her own son. The princess named him Moses, for she explained, "I lifted him out of the water."

Now What?

No one can mess with God's plan. He always accomplishes what he sets out to do. When the Egyptian king ordered that all the baby boys be murdered in order to keep them from growing up to be soldiers, one woman would not obey his order. She couldn't allow her son to be murdered. That was very brave of her. God blessed her by keeping her son alive. Moses grew up to do important work for God. Can you think of ways that God has kept you safe? Do you think he has important work for you to do too?

19

THE BURNING BUSH

What's Up

Moses' mother had known that her son was special. It was true—God had important work for Moses to do. He grew up and became a shepherd, and one day God had a special message for him. God spoke to Moses from a bush that was on fire but never burned up. From this bush, God spoke to Moses and gave him an important job to do.

Action Adventure from Exodus 3:1-18; 4:1-16, 21-23

Moses led the flock [of his father-in-law] into the wilderness and came to Sinai, the mountain of God. The angel of the LORD appeared to him in a fire from the middle of a bush. Moses stared in amazement. Though the bush was in flames, it didn't burn up. God called from the middle of the bush, "Moses! Moses!"

"Here I am!" Moses replied.

"Do not come any closer," the LORD warned. "Take off your sandals, for you are standing on holy ground. I have seen my people in Egypt. I have come to lead them out of Egypt into their own land. I am sending you to Pharaoh. You must lead my people out of Egypt."

But Moses protested, "If I go to the people and tell them, 'The God of your ancestors has sent me to you,' they will ask me, 'What is his name?' What should I tell them?"

God replied, "Say this: I AM has sent me. You and the elders must go to the king of Egypt and tell him, 'The God of the Hebrews has met with us. Let us take a three-day journey into the wilderness to offer sacrifices to the LORD, our God.'"

Moses protested again, "What if they won't believe me or listen to me?"

Key Verse

This is my command—be strong and courageous! Do not be afraid or discouraged. For the LORD your God is with you wherever you go.

Joshua 1:9

The LORD asked him, "What is that in your hand?"

"A shepherd's staff," Moses replied.

"Throw it down on the ground," the LORD told him. Moses threw down the staff, and it turned into a snake!

Then the LORD told him, "Grab its tail." Moses grabbed it, and it turned back into a shepherd's staff.

Then the LORD said, "Put your hand inside your cloak." Moses put his hand inside his cloak, and when he took it out, his hand was white with a skin disease. "Now put your hand back into your cloak," the LORD said. So Moses put his hand back in, and when he took it out again, it was as healthy as the rest of his body.

But Moses pleaded with the LORD, "I'm not very good with words. I get tongue-tied, and my words get tangled."

I'm not sure about this, but God sure sounded SURE!

The LORD became angry with Moses. "Your brother, Aaron, will be your spokesman. Go to Pharaoh and perform the miracles I have empowered you to do. I will harden his heart so he will refuse to let the people go. Then you will tell him, 'The LORD says: Israel is my firstborn son. Let my son go, so he can worship me.'"

Now What?

Maybe being a shepherd didn't seem special to Moses. But that day when the bush started burning, Moses found out God had a job for him. It wasn't an easy job. Moses even tried to talk God out of asking him to do it. But God knew that Moses was his man. Has God ever asked you to do something hard? Maybe he wanted you to take a stand for him with your friends or refuse to do something your friends were doing because you knew it was wrong. Were you scared? Did you ask for his help?

20

PERIL OF THE PLAGUES, PART I

What's Up

God wanted his people to be free from slavery in Egypt, so he sent Moses to talk to Pharaoh. Each time Pharaoh refused to let the Hebrews go, God sent a plague—a terrible trouble that touched the Egyptians. Then Pharaoh begged Moses to take the plague away and promised to let the Hebrews leave. However, when things were okay again, Pharaoh changed his mind. It was clear that he didn't know who he was dealing with!

Action Adventure from Exodus 7:14–8:32

The LORD said to Moses, "Announce to [Pharaoh], 'The LORD says: I will strike the water of the Nile, and the river will turn to blood.'"

Then the LORD said to Moses: "Tell Aaron, 'Take your staff and raise your hand over the waters. Turn all the water to blood. Everywhere in Egypt the water will turn to blood.'"

Moses and Aaron did as the LORD commanded. The fish in the river died, and the water became so foul that the Egyptians couldn't drink it.

The magicians of Egypt used magic, and they, too, turned water into blood. So Pharaoh returned to his palace and put the whole thing out of his mind.

Then the LORD said, "Go back to Pharaoh and announce, 'The LORD says: Let my people go. If you refuse, I will send a plague of frogs. They will come into your palace and onto your bed! They will even jump into your ovens.'"

Then the LORD said, "Tell Aaron, 'Raise the staff over all the rivers and ponds of Egypt, and bring up frogs over all the land.'"

Pharaoh summoned Moses and begged, "Plead with the LORD to take the frogs away. I will let your people go."

Key Verse

The LORD's plans stand firm forever; his intentions can never be shaken.

Psalm 33:11

"All right," Moses replied. "Then you will know that there is no one like the LORD our God." Moses cried out to the LORD and when Pharaoh saw that relief had come, he refused to listen to Moses and Aaron.

So the LORD said, "Tell Aaron, 'Raise your staff and strike the ground.'" When Aaron struck the ground all the dust in the land of Egypt turned into gnats. Pharaoh's magicians tried to do the same thing but this time they failed. But Pharaoh's heart remained hard.

Then the LORD told Moses, "Say to [Pharaoh], 'The LORD says: Let my people go. If you refuse, I will send flies. But this time I will spare the region where my people live. No flies will be found there.'"

The LORD did just as he had said. The whole land of Egypt was thrown into chaos by the flies. Pharaoh called for Moses and Aaron. "Offer sacrifices to

This guy just doesn't get it!

your God," he said. "But do it here in this land."

Moses replied, "If we offer our sacrifices here, the Egyptians will stone us. We must take a trip into the wilderness to offer sacrifices to our God."

"Go ahead," Pharaoh replied.

So Moses pleaded with the LORD to remove the flies. And the LORD did. But Pharaoh again became stubborn and refused to let the people go.

Now What?

Pharaoh thought he could fight God and win. He was wrong. God showed an unbelievable amount of patience with the Egyptian king. God gave him many opportunities to let the Hebrew people leave. God is very patient. He asks us to obey him, to read his Word, to love and serve him. He is patient with us when we fail. Is there any place in your life where you know you have not been obeying God? Do you need to thank God for his patience with you?

21

PERIL OF THE PLAGUES, PART 2

What's Up

Pharaoh was a slow learner. God sent plague after plague, trouble after trouble, to show Pharaoh his power. God wanted Pharaoh to know he was serious about his people being free. Each time a plague came on them, Pharaoh said the Hebrew people could leave. But once the problem was removed, he always changed his mind. As God was watching Pharaoh turn down nine chances to let the people go, God was losing patience with Pharaoh!

Action Adventure from Exodus 9:1-29, 34-35

"Go back to Pharaoh," the LORD commanded Moses. "Tell him, 'God says: Let my people go, so they can worship me. If you refuse to let them go, the LORD will strike all your livestock—horses, donkeys, camels, cattle, sheep, and goats—with a deadly plague. But not a single one of Israel's animals will die!'" The next morning all the livestock of the Egyptians died. The Israelites didn't lose a single animal.

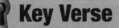

Key Verse

Tell everyone about God's power. His majesty shines down on Israel; his strength is mighty in the heavens.

Psalm 68:34

But Pharaoh's heart remained stubborn, and he still refused to let the people go.

Then the LORD said to Moses, "Take handfuls of soot from a brick kiln, and toss it into the air while Pharaoh watches. The ashes will spread like dust over the whole land of Egypt, causing boils to break out on people and animals throughout the land." Moses threw the soot into the air, and boils broke out on people and animals alike. But the LORD hardened Pharaoh's heart, and just as the LORD had predicted to Moses, Pharaoh refused to listen.

Then the LORD said to Moses, "Stand before Pharaoh. Tell him, 'This is what the God of the Hebrews says: Let my people go, so they can worship me. If you don't, tomorrow at this time I will send a hailstorm.'"

Then the LORD said to Moses, "Lift your hand toward the sky so hail may fall on the people, the livestock, and all the plants throughout the land of Egypt." Moses lifted his staff, and the LORD sent thunder and hail, and lightning flashed toward the earth. The LORD sent a hailstorm against all the land of Egypt. It left all of Egypt in ruins. The hail struck down everything in the open field—people, animals, and plants alike. Even the trees were destroyed. The only place without hail was where the people of Israel lived.

Then Pharaoh quickly summoned Moses and Aaron. "This time I have sinned," he confessed. "The LORD is the righteous one, and my people and I are wrong. Please beg the LORD to end this terrifying thunder and hail. We've had enough. I will let you go; you don't need to stay any longer."

That should get his attention!

Moses replied. "I will lift my hands and pray to the LORD. Then the thunder and hail will stop, and you will know that the earth belongs to the LORD."

But when Pharaoh saw that the rain, hail, and thunder had stopped, Pharaoh again became stubborn. Because his heart was hard, Pharaoh refused to let the people leave, just as the LORD had predicted through Moses.

Now What?

Did Pharaoh think he could outsmart God? Did he think he could trick him? Nine times he lied to God. Each time God gave him another chance, while still showing his awesome power. Are you trying to trick God by saying you will change something in your life . . . but then not following through? You can see from this story that God doesn't give up, and you can't fool him. So why not tell God today that you WILL obey . . . then do it!

22

PREPARING FOR PASSOVER

What's Up

Pharaoh had nine times to listen to God. Now he had run out of times. God would send a 10th plague, and this one would be so terrible that Pharaoh would finally listen. But God wanted to be sure his people would be safe from this plague. He gave them directions, telling them what to do to be safe. So now it was the Hebrews' turn to obey.

Action Adventure from Exodus 11:1, 5; 12:1-7, 21-23, 28-31, 37-42

The LORD said to Moses, "I will strike the land of Egypt with one more blow. All the firstborn sons will die in every family in Egypt, from the oldest son of Pharaoh to the oldest son of his lowliest servant girl."

The LORD gave the following instructions to Moses and Aaron: "Each family must choose a lamb or a young goat for a sacrifice, one animal for each household. The animal you select must be a one-year-old male, either a sheep or a goat, with no defects. They are to take some of the blood and smear it on the sides and top of the doorframes of the houses where they eat the animal."

Then Moses called all the elders of Israel together and said to them, "Pick out a lamb or young goat for each of your families, and slaughter the Passover animal. Then take a bundle of hyssop branches and dip it into the blood. Brush the hyssop across the top and sides of the doorframes of your houses. For the LORD will pass through the land to strike down the Egyptians. But when he sees the blood on the top and sides of the doorframe, the LORD will pass over your home. He will not permit his death angel to enter your house and strike you down."

Key Verse

Seek the Kingdom of God above all else, and live righteously, and he will give you everything you need.

Matthew 6:33

The people of Israel did just as the LORD had commanded through Moses and Aaron. And that night at midnight, the LORD struck down all the firstborn sons in the land of Egypt, from the firstborn son of Pharaoh, who sat on his throne, to the firstborn son of the prisoner. Even the firstborn of their livestock were killed. Pharaoh and all his officials and all the people of Egypt woke up during the night, and loud wailing was heard throughout the land of Egypt. There was not a single house where someone had not died.

Pharaoh sent for Moses and Aaron during the night. "Get out!" he ordered. "Leave my people—and take the rest of the Israelites with you!"

That night the people of Israel left Rameses and started

I think he finally got the message!

for Succoth. There were about 600,000 men, plus all the women and children.

The people of Israel had lived in Egypt for 430 years. In fact, it was on the last day of the 430th year that all the LORD's forces left the land. On this night the LORD kept his promise to bring his people out of the land of Egypt.

Now What?

God wants his children to obey him because he knows what is best for the ones he loves. The Hebrews had to obey God's directions in order to be safe from the last terrible plague. They couldn't rush ahead in panic. They couldn't turn and run. They had to go step-by-step and do what God said. That took trust. Do you trust God, even when you are afraid? Do you trust him enough to obey him even when you can't see how his plan is going to work out?

23

DANGER AT THE RED SEA

What's Up

Pharaoh just did not learn. Even after the terrible 10th plague, he changed his mind again and began to chase the Hebrews. He wanted to bring them back to slavery! But God had been leading his people during the day by a tall cloud pillar. At night he sent a tall fire pillar to give them light. God didn't lead his people out of Egypt just to let them be rounded up and taken back. He had a plan, and there was no way Pharaoh was going to win!

Action Adventure from Exodus 14:5-14, 19-28

Pharaoh and his officials changed their minds. "What have we done, letting all those Israelite slaves get away?" they asked. So Pharaoh harnessed his chariot and called up his troops. He took with him 600 of Egypt's best chariots. He chased after the people of Israel.

The people of Israel saw the Egyptians overtaking them. They said to Moses, "Why did you bring us out here to die in the wilderness? Weren't there enough graves for us in Egypt? Didn't we tell you this would happen? We said, 'It's better to be a slave in Egypt than a corpse in the wilderness!'"

But Moses told the people, "Don't be afraid. Just stand still and watch the LORD rescue you today. The Egyptians you see today will never be seen again. The LORD himself will fight for you. Just stay calm." Then the angel of God, who had been leading the people of Israel, moved to the rear of the camp. The pillar of cloud also moved from the front and stood behind them. The cloud settled between the Egyptian and Israelite camps. As darkness fell, the cloud turned to fire, lighting up the night. But the Egyptians and

Key Verse

Moses told the people, "Don't be afraid. Just stand still and watch the LORD rescue you today."

Exodus 14:13

Israelites did not approach each other all night.

Then Moses raised his hand over the sea, and the LORD opened up a path through the water with a strong east wind. The wind blew all that night, turning the seabed into dry land. So the people of Israel walked through the middle of the sea on dry ground, with walls of water on each side!

Then the Egyptians chased them into the middle of the sea. But just before dawn the LORD looked down on the Egyptian army from the pillar of fire and cloud. He twisted their chariot wheels, making their chariots difficult to drive. "Let's get out of here!" the Egyptians shouted. "The LORD is fighting for them against Egypt!"

When all the Israelites had reached the other side, the LORD said to Moses, "Raise your hand over the sea again. Then

I'll say this for him: he doesn't give up.

the waters will rush back and cover the Egyptians and their chariots." So as the sun began to rise, Moses raised his hand over the sea, and the water rushed back into its usual place. The Egyptians tried to escape, but the LORD swept them into the sea. Of all the Egyptians who had chased the Israelites into the sea, not a single one survived.

Now What?

It's easy to trust God when things are going well. It's even easy to trust him in difficult times when you can see the answer to your prayers on the way. But when you can't see any possible answer to how God is going to take care of you, it's harder to trust. That's where the Hebrews were. They probably never dreamed that God would part the waters to give them a safe escape. Can you trust enough to believe that nothing is impossible with God?

24

CLOUDY WITH A CHANCE OF MANNA

What's Up

God sent 10 plagues to convince Pharaoh he should let the Hebrews leave Egypt. Then he parted the waters of the Red Sea to keep God's people safe from the Egyptian army. It was clear that God wanted his people to be free. So would he send them into the wilderness just to let them die of hunger? The Hebrews must have thought so because they started to be upset and cry. However, once again, God showed them his power and his love. He provided what they needed right when they needed it.

Action Adventure from Exodus 16:1-31

Israel journeyed into the wilderness between Elim and Mount Sinai. There the whole community complained about Moses and Aaron. "If only the LORD had killed us back in Egypt," they moaned. "You have brought us into this wilderness to starve us to death."

Then the LORD said to Moses, "I'm going to rain down food from heaven. I will test [the people] to see whether or not they will follow my instructions."

So Moses and Aaron said to Israel, "In the morning you will see the glory of the LORD, because he has heard your complaints, which are against him, not against us. The LORD will give you meat to eat in the evening and bread to satisfy you in the morning."

Then the LORD said to Moses, "In the evening you will have meat to eat, and in the morning you will have all the bread you want. Then you will know that I am the LORD your God." That evening vast numbers of quail flew in and covered the camp. And the next morning the area around the camp was wet with dew. When the dew evaporated, a flaky substance blanketed the ground. The Israelites were

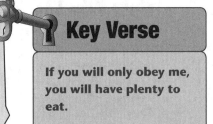

Key Verse

If you will only obey me, you will have plenty to eat.

Isaiah 1:19

puzzled when they saw it. "What is it?" they asked.

Moses told them, "It is the food the LORD has given you. These are the LORD's instructions: Each household should pick up two quarts for each person in your tent." Some gathered a lot, some only a little. Each family had just what it needed. Then Moses told them, "Do not keep any of it until morning." But some of them didn't listen and kept some until morning. By then it was full of maggots and had a terrible smell.

After this the people gathered the food morning by morning, each family according to its need. And as the sun became hot, the flakes they had not picked up melted and disappeared. On the sixth day, Moses told them, "Tomorrow will be a holy Sabbath day set apart for the LORD. So bake or boil as much as you want today, and set aside what is left for tomorrow."

He said to take only what we need. After what I saw at the Red Sea, I'm obeying!

So they put some aside until morning, just as Moses had commanded. And in the morning the leftover food was good, without maggots or odor. Some of the people went out anyway on the seventh day, but they found no food. The LORD asked Moses, "How long will these people refuse to obey?"

The Israelites called the food manna.

Now What?

How many times did God have to show his love and care for the Hebrews before they would trust him? Apparently he always had to do it just one more time! Their faith did not run very deep in their hearts. This story is both a lesson of trusting God and of obeying his directions, because the two things go hand in hand. If you obey God, you see him care for you. If you don't obey, you see how he corrects you. Do you obey? Do you see God's care? Does that help you trust more?

25

THE TEN COMMANDMENTS

What's Up

God spoke to Moses and gave him 10 rules called "commandments" to pass along to the people. These commandments would help them treat one another well and get along together. The commandments also taught them how to relate to God. We know these commands as the Ten Commandments. God gave them out of love for his people. But were they received that way?

Action Adventure from Exodus 19:1–20:17

After the Israelites left Egypt, they set up camp at the base of Mount Sinai. Moses climbed the mountain to appear before God. The LORD said, "Give these instructions to the family of Jacob: 'If you will obey me, you will be my own special treasure from among all the peoples on earth. And you will be my holy nation.'"

So Moses called together the people and told them everything the LORD had commanded. The people responded, "We will do everything the LORD has commanded."

Then the LORD said to Moses, "I will come to you in a thick cloud so the people can hear me when I speak with you. Go down and prepare the people for my arrival. Be sure they are ready on the third day, for on that day the LORD will come down on Mount Sinai. Warn the people, 'Be careful! Do not go up on the mountain or even touch its boundaries. Anyone who touches the mountain will be put to death.' However, when the ram's horn sounds a long blast, then the people may go up on the mountain."

On the morning of the third day, there was a long, loud blast from a ram's horn, and all the people trembled. Moses led them out to meet with God, and they

Key Verse

If you will obey me and keep my covenant, you will be my own special treasure from among all the peoples on earth; for all the earth belongs to me. And you will be my kingdom of priests, my holy nation.

Exodus 19:5-6

stood at the foot of the mountain. All of Mount Sinai was covered with smoke because the LORD had descended on it in the form of fire. The smoke billowed into the sky, and the whole mountain shook. As the blast of the ram's horn grew louder, Moses spoke, and God thundered his reply. The LORD came down on the top of Mount Sinai and called Moses to the top of the mountain.

He really knows how to get a guy's attention!

The LORD said, "Go down and bring Aaron back up with you. In the meantime, do not let the priests or the people break through to approach the LORD, or he will break out and destroy them."

Then God gave these instructions:

"I am the LORD your God. You must not have any other god but me.

You must not make for yourself an idol of any kind.

You must not misuse the name of the LORD your God.

Remember to observe the Sabbath day by keeping it holy.

Honor your father and mother.

You must not murder.

You must not commit adultery.

You must not steal.

You must not testify falsely against your neighbor.

You must not covet anything that belongs to your neighbor."

Now What?

Four of the Ten Commandments teach God's people how to treat God. He is to be Number One in people's lives. And he is to be treated with love and respect. The other six commandments teach us how to get along with other people. These may seem simple, but there are often one or two that are harder for each person to obey. Do you especially struggle with one or two of the Ten Commandments? Ask God for help to do what is right. He will help you!

26

GOLDEN CALF MESS-UP

What's Up

Let's review what the Hebrews had seen God do. He had sent 10 plagues to get them out of Egypt, had parted the Red Sea to keep them safe, and had sent food from heaven to feed them. But they still did not believe he was leading them and taking care of them. They knew that Moses was up on the mountain talking with God, but they got tired of waiting for him to come back. They wanted quick action. So, once again they showed they did not have faith in God—they didn't trust in him.

Action Adventure from Exodus 32:1-24, 29-34

When the people saw how long it was taking Moses to come back down the mountain, they gathered around Aaron. They said, "Make us gods who can lead us. We don't know what happened to Moses."

Aaron said, "Take the gold rings from the ears of your wives and sons and daughters and bring them to me."

🔑 Key Verse

You must not have any other god but me . . . for I, the LORD your God, am a jealous God who will not tolerate your affection for any other gods.

Exodus 20:3, 5

Aaron took the gold, melted it, and molded it into the shape of a calf. When the people saw it, they exclaimed, "O Israel, these are the gods who brought you out of Egypt!"

The LORD told Moses, "Your people have turned away from the way I commanded them to live! They have melted gold and made a calf and sacrificed to it. They are saying, 'These are your gods, O Israel, who brought you out of Egypt.' I have seen how stubborn these people are. I will destroy them."

Moses said. "Why are you so angry? Change your mind about this terrible disaster you have threatened against your people! Remember your servants Abraham, Isaac, and Jacob."

So the LORD changed his mind. Then Moses went down the mountain. He held the two stone tablets with the terms of the covenant. The words on them were written by God himself.

When Moses saw the calf, he burned with anger. He threw the stone tablets to the ground, smashing them. He took the calf and burned it, ground it into powder, threw it into the water, and forced the people to drink it. Finally, he turned to Aaron and demanded, "What did these people do to make you bring such terrible sin upon them?"

Aaron replied, "They said, 'Make us gods who will lead us.' So I told them, 'Whoever has gold jewelry, take it off.' When they brought it to me, I threw it into the fire—and out came this calf!"

The next day Moses said to the people, "You have committed a terrible sin, but I will go back

Haven't you heard of "righteous indignation"?

to the LORD. Perhaps I will be able to obtain forgiveness for your sin."

Moses returned to the LORD and said, "What a terrible sin these people have committed. If you will only forgive their sin."

The LORD replied, "I will erase the name of everyone who has sinned against me. When I come to call the people to account, I will hold them responsible for their sins."

Now What?

God will not share first place in his children's hearts with anything or anyone else. There is a reason for that—it is impossible to have two (or more) people or things in charge of your life. You either serve God with all your heart or not at all. You can't give only part of your heart to God and give the rest of it to things that God says are not right. You're all or nothing for God. What is most important to you? God or ___? Choose God and live for him!

27

ISRAEL'S BIG MISTAKE

What's Up

When God led his people out of Egypt, he promised to give them their own land so they would have a place to call home. But he expected them to do their part so they could possess the land. He told Moses to send spies into the land to see what it was like. The spies' report should not have frightened the people. They knew that God had already promised to give the land to them. But once again the faith of the Israelites was weak.

Action Adventure from Numbers 13:1-2, 21-28, 33; 14:1-21, 27-30

The LORD said to Moses, "Send men to explore the land I am giving to the Israelites."

So [the men] explored the land. They cut a branch with a cluster of grapes so large that it took two of them to carry it on a pole between them!

After exploring the land for forty days, the men returned.

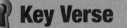

Key Verse

Do not rebel against the LORD, and don't be afraid of the people of the land. They are only helpless prey to us! They have no protection, but the LORD is with us! Don't be afraid of them!

Numbers 14:9

This was their report: "It is a land flowing with milk and honey. Here is the kind of fruit it produces. But the people are powerful, and their towns are large. We even saw giants there. Next to them we felt like grasshoppers!"

The whole community cried in protest against Moses and Aaron. "If only we had died in Egypt! Why is the LORD taking us to this country only to have us die in battle? Let's choose a new leader and go back to Egypt!"

Two men who had explored the land, Joshua and Caleb, said, "The LORD will bring us safely into that rich land flowing with milk and honey. Do not be afraid of the people. The LORD is with us!"

But the whole community began to talk about stoning Joshua and Caleb. Then the LORD appeared to the Israelites and said to Moses, "Will these people never believe me, even after all the miraculous signs I have done among them? I will destroy them."

But Moses objected. "What will the Egyptians think when they hear about it?" he asked the LORD. "They know the power you displayed in rescuing your people. If you slaughter these people, the nations that have heard of your fame will say, 'The LORD was not able to bring them into the land he swore to give them.'

"Please, Lord, prove that your power is great. For you said, 'The LORD is slow to anger and filled with unfailing love, forgiving every kind of sin.' Please pardon the sins of this people."

With a little hard work and the Lord's help, we can do it!

The LORD said, "I will pardon them. But I have heard the complaints the Israelites are making against me. Tell them this: 'Because you complained against me, every one of you who is twenty years or older will not enter the land. The only exceptions will be Caleb and Joshua.'"

Now What?

The bottom line is that the Israelites didn't believe God would do what he said he would do. But God is not like a person, changing his mind every other minute. God said he would give his people the new land, and he meant it. It must have made his heart sad when the people didn't believe him . . . again. You may want to look up a few promises God has made to you in his Word (examples: Numbers 23:19; Psalm 32:8; John 3:16; Romans 8:28-29). Which ones do you believe? Ask for God's help to believe all of his promises.

28

WHAT THE DONKEY SAID

What's Up

King Balak wanted to get rid of the Israelites. Their numbers were growing, and he was afraid of them. He thought they might try to take over his country. So he sent for Balaam to come and put a curse on them. Now, Balaam served God. He knew better than to make plans to do what he wanted rather than what God wanted. But in his heart he did just that. So God had to get his attention in an unusual way!

Action Adventure from Numbers 22:1-35

The people of Israel traveled to Moab. When the people of Moab saw how many Israelites there were, they were terrified.

So Balak, king of Moab, sent messengers to Balaam. His message said: "Come and curse these people. Then I will be able to drive them from the land."

"Stay here overnight," Balaam said. "In the morning I will tell you whatever the LORD directs me to say."

God told Balaam, "You are not to curse these people, for they have been blessed!"

The next morning Balaam told Balak's officials, "The LORD will not let me go with you."

Balak tried again. He sent a larger number of officials. They delivered this message: "This is what Balak says: I will pay you very well. Just come!"

Balaam responded, "I would be powerless to do anything against the will of God. But stay here one more night, and I will see if the LORD has anything else to say to me."

That night God told him, "Go with them. But do only what I tell you to do." So the next morning Balaam started off with the officials. But God was angry that Balaam was going, so he sent the angel of the LORD to block his way. Balaam's donkey saw the angel standing in the road with a sword in his hand. The donkey bolted off the road,

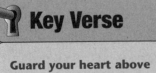

Key Verse

Guard your heart above all else, for it determines the course of your life.

Proverbs 4:23

but Balaam beat it and turned it back onto the road. Then the angel stood at a place where the road narrowed between two walls. When the donkey saw the angel, it tried to squeeze by and crushed Balaam's foot against the wall. So Balaam beat the donkey again. Then the angel moved farther down the road and stood in a place too narrow for the donkey to get by. When the donkey saw the angel, it lay down. Balaam beat the animal again.

Wow! If I knew you could talk, I would have joined the circus.

Then the LORD gave the donkey the ability to speak. "What have I done that deserves your beating me three times? I am the same donkey you have ridden all your life. Have I ever done anything like this before?"

"No," Balaam admitted.

Then the LORD opened Balaam's eyes, and he saw the angel of the LORD. Balaam bowed his head and fell on the ground. Balaam confessed, "I have sinned. I didn't realize you were standing in the road. I will return home if you are against my going."

But the angel told Balaam, "Go, but say only what I tell you to say."

Now What?

When you read this story, do you wonder about it? Does it seem as though Balaam was obeying God? After all, he prayed and waited for God's answer before going with the messengers. Well, the thing to remember is that God sees more than our actions. He also sees what is going on inside our hearts. He knew that in Balaam's heart Balaam was not obeying him. Your actions can make it appear that you are obeying God, but he knows all the reasons why you do what you do!

29

RAHAB AND THE SPIES

What's Up

Joshua sent spies into Jericho to check out the city that God had promised to give the Israelites. A woman in the city knew who the spies were. She believed in their God. So she would not help the king of Jericho. She even put her own life in danger to keep the spies safe. She believed that much in God and his power. The spies agreed in return for her help to keep her and her family safe when the Israelite army came to destroy the city.

Action Adventure from Joshua 2

Joshua sent out two spies. He instructed them, "Scout out the land on the other side of the Jordan River, especially around Jericho." So the two men set out and came to the house of Rahab and stayed there that night.

But someone told the king of Jericho, "Some Israelites have come here tonight to spy out the land." So the king sent orders to Rahab: "Bring out the men who have come into your house."

Rahab replied, "The men were here earlier, but I didn't know where they were from. They left the town. I don't know where they went. If you hurry, you can probably catch up with them." (Actually, she had taken them up to the roof and hidden them beneath bundles of flax.)

Before the spies went to sleep, Rahab went to talk with them. "I know the LORD has given you this land," she told them. "We are all afraid of you. For the LORD your God is the supreme God of the heavens above and the earth below. Swear to me that you will be kind to me and my family since I have helped you. Give me some guarantee that when Jericho is conquered, you will let me live, along with my [family]."

"We offer our own lives as a guarantee for your safety," the men agreed. "If you don't betray

Key Verse

Be strong and courageous, all you who put your hope in the LORD!

Psalm 31:24

us, we will keep our promise and be kind to you when the LORD gives us the land."

Then, since Rahab's house was built into the town wall, she let them down by a rope through the window.

Before they left, the men told her, "We will be bound by the oath we have taken only if you follow these instructions. When we come into the land, you must leave this scarlet rope hanging from the window. All your family members must be here inside the house. If anyone lays a hand on people inside this house, we will accept the responsibility for their death. If you betray us, however, we are not bound by this oath in any way."

"I accept your terms," she replied. And she sent them on

I hope you guys remember what the rope means.

their way, leaving the scarlet rope hanging from the window.

Then the two spies reported to Joshua all that had happened to them. "The LORD has given us the whole land," they said, "for all the people in the land are terrified of us."

Now What?

Rahab took a chance. If the king of Jericho had found out she lied to him about the spies, she probably would have been killed. But she believed so strongly in the power of the Israelites' God that she was willing to take that chance. How deep is your belief in who God is and how powerful he is? Are you willing to stand up for him in some of the hardest places—like in front of your friends? Are you happy to let people know you trust God? Do you have the courage of Rahab?

30

CROSSING THE JORDAN

What's Up

The Israelite people could see that God was leading them, even though their faith was often weak. God wanted them to know that he had chosen Joshua to be their leader and that he was with Joshua. As part of God's plan, the priests would be carrying the Ark of the Covenant. This was a gold box with two angels on top. Inside were the Ten Commandments, a jar of manna, and Aaron's staff—all to remind God's people that he was with them, ready to do more miracles!

Action Adventure from Joshua 3:1–4:7, 14

The next morning Joshua and the Israelites arrived at the Jordan River, where they camped. Three days later the Israelite officers went through the camp, giving these instructions to the people: "When you see the priests carrying the Ark of the Covenant, follow them. Stay about a half mile behind them."

The LORD told Joshua, "Today I will begin to make you a great leader in the eyes of the Israelites. They will know that I am with you, just as I was with Moses. Give this command to the priests who carry the Ark of the Covenant: 'When you reach the banks of the Jordan River, take a few steps into the river and stop there.'"

So Joshua told the Israelites, "The Ark of the Covenant will lead you across the Jordan River! The priests will carry the Ark. As soon as their feet touch the water, the flow of water will be cut off upstream, and the river will stand up like a wall."

So the people left their camp to cross the Jordan, and the priests who were carrying the Ark of the Covenant went ahead of them. The Jordan was overflowing its banks. But as soon as the feet of the priests

🔑 Key Verse

We are God's masterpiece. He has created us anew in Christ Jesus, so we can do the good things he planned for us long ago.

Ephesians 2:10

who were carrying the Ark touched the water, the water above that point began backing up. The water below that point flowed on to the Dead Sea until the riverbed was dry. Then all the people crossed over near the town of Jericho. Meanwhile, the priests who were carrying the Ark stood on dry ground in the middle of the riverbed as the people passed. They waited there until the whole nation of Israel had crossed the Jordan on dry ground.

When all the people had crossed, the LORD said to Joshua, "Now choose twelve men, one from each tribe. Tell them, 'Take twelve stones from the place where the priests are standing in the middle of the Jordan.'" Joshua told [the twelve men], "Each of you must pick up one stone—one for each of the twelve tribes of Israel. We will build a memorial. In the future

This will show them who's boss!

your children will ask, 'What do these stones mean?' Tell them, 'They remind us that the Jordan River stopped flowing when the Ark of the LORD's Covenant went across.'"

That day the LORD made Joshua a great leader in the eyes of all the Israelites, and for the rest of his life they revered him as much as they had revered Moses.

Now What?

It's pretty cool that God had a plan for Joshua and for the whole Israelite nation. There probably were times when Joshua wondered if God's plan was happening. There also must have been times when the Israelites wondered about it. So once in a while God did an amazing miracle to remind them that he was still working. Are there times when you wonder if God really is working on a plan for you? He is, and even if you can't see how he is doing it right now, he will keep working and showing you his plan. Enjoy the journey!

31

JUDGMENT AT JERICHO

What's Up

Nothing is impossible when God is in control. It might have seemed as if there would be no way for Joshua's army to break through the high, thick walls around the city of Jericho. But God had a plan. As long as Joshua did what God told him to do, the people of Jericho didn't have a chance. Joshua listened to God and obeyed, and the rest is history!

Action Adventure from Joshua 6

Now the gates of Jericho were tightly shut because the people were afraid of the Israelites. No one was allowed to go out or in. But the LORD said to Joshua, "I have given you Jericho. You and your fighting men should march around the town once a day for six days. Seven priests will walk ahead of the Ark, each carrying a ram's horn. On the seventh day you are to march around the town seven times, with the priests blowing the horns. When you hear the priests give one long blast on the rams' horns, have all the people shout as loud as they can. Then the walls of the town will collapse, and the people can charge straight into the town."

So Joshua called together the priests and said, "Take up the Ark of the Covenant, and assign seven priests to walk in front of it, each carrying a ram's horn." Then he gave orders to the people: "March around the town, and the armed men will lead the way in front of the Ark. Do not shout; do not even talk. Not a single word from any of you until I tell you to shout. Then shout!" So the Ark was carried around the town once that day.

Joshua got up early the next morning, and the priests again carried the Ark of the LORD. The seven priests with the rams' horns marched in front of the Ark of the LORD, blowing their horns. Again the armed men marched both in front of the priests and

Key Verse

Royal power belongs to the LORD. He rules all the nations.

Psalm 22:28

behind the Ark. All this time the priests were blowing their horns. On the second day they again marched around the town once and returned to the camp. They followed this pattern for six days.

On the seventh day the Israelites marched around the town seven times. The seventh time around, as the priests sounded the long blast on their horns, Joshua commanded the people, "Shout! For the LORD has given you the town! Jericho and everything in it must be completely destroyed. Only Rahab and the others in her house will be spared, for she protected our spies."

When the people heard the sound of the horns, they shouted as loud as they could. The

Hurry up! This is going to get really ugly.

walls of Jericho collapsed, and the Israelites charged straight into the town and captured it. The men who had been spies brought out Rahab. They moved her whole family to a safe place.

The LORD was with Joshua, and his reputation spread throughout the land.

Now What?

The king of Jericho thought his power was strong enough to fight God. He was wrong. Some people still think that being rich or famous or powerful makes them more important than God. They are wrong too. You may think it will help you to listen to the opinion of friends or classmates who think they are very cool. Remember that their opinion of you does not matter as much as God's opinion. Choosing to obey him is better than trying to do what others think you should do. If you make God number one in your life, no one else will have more power over you than he does.

32

ACHAN BLOWS IT

What's Up

God gave exact directions to Joshua and his people about what to do when they took over cities. However, one man, Achan, did not obey God's directions. He thought God wouldn't notice that he didn't obey. He thought it was a secret. He was wrong. There are no secrets from God. So things had to be made right or the Israelites would have no more victories!

Action Adventure from Joshua 7:1-25; 8:1-3, 28

A man named Achan had stolen some of these things [that were dedicated to the LORD], so the LORD was angry. Joshua sent some men to spy out the town of Ai. When they returned, they told Joshua, "It won't take more than two or three thousand men to attack Ai. Since there are so few of them, don't make all our people struggle to go up there." So approximately 3,000 warriors were sent, but they were defeated.

Joshua and the elders of Israel tore their clothing, threw dust on their heads, and bowed face down to the ground before the Ark of the LORD until evening. Then Joshua cried out, "Oh, LORD, why did you bring us across the Jordan River if you are going to let the Amorites kill us?"

But the LORD said, "Get up! Israel has sinned! They have stolen things. They have lied about it and hidden the things. Hidden among you are things set apart for the LORD. You will never defeat your enemies until you remove these things. The one who has stolen has broken the covenant of the LORD."

The next morning Joshua brought the tribes of Israel before

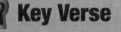

Key Verse

Don't make judgments about anyone ahead of time—before the Lord returns. For he will bring our darkest secrets to light and will reveal our private motives. Then God will give to each one whatever praise is due.

1 Corinthians 4:5

the LORD, and the tribe of Judah was singled out. Then the clan of Zerah was singled out. Then the family of Zimri was singled out. Every member of Zimri's family was brought forward, and Achan was singled out.

Joshua said to Achan, "Give glory to the LORD by telling the truth."

Achan replied, "I have sinned against the LORD. I saw a robe from Babylon, 200 silver coins, and a bar of gold. I wanted them so much that I took them. They are hidden in the ground beneath my tent."

Joshua sent some men to search. They found the stolen goods hidden, just as Achan had said. They brought them to Joshua. Then they laid them on the ground in the presence of the LORD. Joshua and all the Israelites took Achan to the valley of Achor. Joshua said, "Why have you brought trouble on us? The LORD will now bring

Wow! They take this really seriously!

trouble on you." All the Israelites stoned Achan.

Then the LORD said to Joshua, "Do not be afraid or discouraged. Take your fighting men and attack Ai, for I have given you the king of Ai, his people, his town, and his land."

Joshua chose 30,000 of his best warriors and sent them out. Joshua burned the town of Ai, and it became a permanent mound of ruins.

Now What?

Perhaps Achan thought he had gotten away with something. He took the treasures and hid them away. No one saw him, so he thought no one knew. However, he couldn't keep his secret from God. He should have known that. It's a good lesson for you, too. You may be able to hide your actions from your parents or friends, but you never can hide them from God. So, don't do anything that you wouldn't want God to know about. He knows.

33

THE SUN STANDS STILL

What's Up

Joshua was the leader of God's army of Israelites. Kings of other nations were afraid of the Israelites because they knew God helped them. Those kings banded together to attack the Gibeonites, who had made peace with the Israelites. The Gibeonites called for Joshua and his army to come help them win the battle. Joshua agreed to help, and God stepped in to do something that seemed impossible!

Action Adventure from Joshua 10:1-14

Adoni-zedek, king of Jerusalem, heard that Joshua had captured and completely destroyed Ai, just as he had destroyed the town of Jericho. He also learned that the Gibeonites had made peace with Israel. He and his people became very afraid when they heard all this because Gibeon was a large town—as large as the royal cities and larger than Ai. And the Gibeonite men were strong warriors.

So King Adoni-zedek sent messengers to several other kings. "Come and help me destroy Gibeon," he urged them, "for they have made peace with Joshua and the people of Israel." So these five Amorite kings combined their armies. They moved all their troops into place and attacked Gibeon.

The men of Gibeon quickly sent messengers to Joshua at his camp in Gilgal. "Don't abandon your servants now!" they pleaded. "Come at once! Help us! For all the Amorite kings who live in the hill country have joined forces to attack us."

So Joshua and his entire army left Gilgal and set out for Gibeon. "Do not be afraid of them," the LORD said to Joshua, "for I have given you victory over them. Not a single one of them will be able to stand up to you."

🔑 Key Verse

Tell everyone about God's power. His . . . strength is mighty in the heavens.

Psalm 68:34

78

Joshua traveled all night from Gilgal and took the Amorite armies by surprise. The LORD threw them into a panic, and the Israelites slaughtered great numbers of them at Gibeon. Then the Israelites chased the enemy along the road to Beth-horon, killing them all along the way. As the Amorites retreated, the LORD destroyed them with a terrible hailstorm from heaven. The hail killed more of the enemy than the Israelites killed with the sword.

On the day the LORD gave the Israelites victory over the Amorites, Joshua prayed to the LORD in front of all the people of Israel. He said, "Let the sun stand still over Gibeon, and the moon over the valley of Aijalon."

So the sun stood still and the moon stayed in place until the nation of Israel had defeated its enemies. The sun stayed in the middle of the sky, and it did not set as on a normal day. There has never been a day like this one before or since, when the LORD answered such a prayer. Surely the LORD fought for Israel that day!

This hardly seems fair!

Now What?

God is the God of miracles. He fights for his people and will do whatever is necessary to protect them or to give them victory over their enemies. Joshua saw God do these things over and over again. And when God caused the sun to stand still, his power was clear to everyone. Even Israel's enemies had to admit his power on that day. Does it make you feel pretty special to have God on your side? It should. His love surrounds you, and his power will fight for you!

34

DEBORAH GOES TO WAR

What's Up

Most of the Israelite leaders named in the Bible are men. But then along came Deborah. She was a prophet—God spoke to her. He gave her the news that he was going to give Israel victory over one of their worst enemies. God wanted Barak to lead his army against Sisera. But Barak wouldn't do it unless Deborah went with him. Because he was a coward, he would not have the honor of winning the battle against Israel's enemy.

Action Adventure from Judges 4

The Israelites again did evil in the LORD's sight. So the LORD turned them over to Jabin, a Canaanite king. The commander of his army was Sisera, who had 900 iron chariots. The people of Israel cried out to the LORD for help.

Deborah was a prophet at that time. One day she sent for Barak. She said, "This is what the God of Israel commands: Call out 10,000 warriors. I will call Sisera to the Kishon River. There I will give you victory over him."

Barak told her, "I will go, but only if you go with me."

"Very well," she replied, "I will go with you. But you will receive no honor, for the LORD's victory over Sisera will be at the hands of a woman." So Barak called together the 10,000 warriors. Deborah went with him.

When Sisera was told that Barak had gone up to Mount Tabor, he called for all 900 of his iron chariots and all of his warriors, and they marched to the Kishon River.

Deborah said to Barak, "Get ready! This is the day the LORD will give you victory over Sisera." So Barak led his 10,000 warriors down the slopes of Mount Tabor into battle. When Barak attacked, the LORD threw Sisera

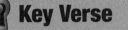

Key Verse

The LORD is my light and my salvation—so why should I be afraid? The LORD is my fortress, protecting me from danger, so why should I tremble?

Psalm 27:1

and all his chariots and warriors into a panic. Sisera leaped down from his chariot and escaped on foot. Barak chased the chariots and the enemy army, killing all of Sisera's warriors.

Meanwhile, Sisera ran to the tent of Jael. She said to him, "Come into my tent. Don't be afraid." So he went into her tent, and she covered him with a blanket.

"Please give me water," he said. "I'm thirsty." So she gave him some milk from a leather bag and covered him again. "Stand at the door of the tent," he told her. "If anybody comes and asks you if there is anyone here, say no."

But when Sisera fell asleep, Jael quietly crept up to him with a hammer and tent peg in her hand. Then she drove the tent peg through his temple and into the ground, and so he died.

Don't worry. I'll take care of you!

When Barak came looking for Sisera, Jael said, "I will show you the man you are looking for." So he followed her into the tent and found Sisera lying there dead.

On that day Israel saw God defeat Jabin. And from that time on Israel became stronger and stronger against King Jabin until they finally destroyed him.

Fear kept Barak from doing the job God asked him to do. But God always gets his work done somehow. He worked through a woman named Jael to accomplish what he wanted. Have you ever been afraid to do a job or a project that you were asked to do? Did God call someone else to do it instead? Think about the good things you may be missing when you are afraid to do a job you have been given. If you learn to trust God and call on his strength to give you courage, you may get to be a part of some amazing experiences!

Now What?

35

GIDEON THE GREAT?

What's Up

The Israelites had many enemies. When they were captured by the Midianites, God called Gideon to free his people. But Gideon couldn't believe that he was the one God chose. He asked for proof, and God gave him that. Then, when Gideon called his army together, God had him send some soldiers home. God kept cutting the size of the army because he wanted everyone to know that victory over the enemy came from his power alone.

Action Adventure from Judges 6:1, 11-16, 33-40; 7:1-9, 16-20

The Israelites did evil in the LORD's sight. So the LORD handed them over to the Midianites for seven years.

Gideon was threshing wheat at the bottom of a winepress. The angel of the LORD appeared to him and said, "Mighty hero, the LORD is with you! Rescue Israel from the Midianites. I will be with you. You will destroy the Midianites as if you were fighting against one man."

The armies of Midian, Amalek, and the people of the east formed an alliance against Israel and crossed the Jordan. Gideon said to God, "If you are going to use me to rescue Israel, prove it. I will put a wool fleece on the threshing floor tonight. If the fleece is wet with dew in the morning but the ground is dry, then I will know that you are going to help me." That is just what happened.

Then Gideon said to God, "Let me use the fleece for one more test. This time let the fleece remain dry while the ground around it is wet." God did as Gideon asked. The fleece was dry in the morning, but the ground was covered with dew.

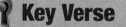

Key Verse

You belong to God, my dear children. You have already won a victory over those people, because the Spirit who lives in you is greater than the spirit who lives in the world.

1 John 4:4

So Gideon and his army went as far as the spring of Harod. The LORD said, "You have too many warriors. Tell the people, 'Whoever is afraid may go home.'" So 22,000 went home, leaving 10,000 to fight.

But the LORD told Gideon, "There are still too many! Divide the men into two groups. In one group put all those who cup water in their hands and lap it up. In the other group put those who kneel down and drink with their mouths." Only 300 of the men drank from their hands. The LORD told Gideon, "With these 300 men I will give you victory over the Midianites. Send all the others home."

That night the LORD said, "Go down into the Midianite camp, for I have given you victory over them!"

[Gideon] divided the men into three groups and gave each man a horn and a jar with a torch in it. Then he said, "Keep your eyes on me. As soon as I

This is a really strange way to fight a battle!

blow the rams' horns, blow your horns, too, and shout, 'For the LORD and for Gideon!'"

It was just after midnight when Gideon and the 100 men with him reached the edge of the Midianite camp. Suddenly, they broke their jars. Then all three groups blew their horns and broke their jars. They held the blazing torches in their left hands and the horns in their right hands, and they all shouted, "A sword for the LORD and for Gideon!"

Now What?

Gideon needed proof from God that he was God's choice to lead the Israelites over the Midianites. God gave him the proof—two times! Then God wanted Gideon's army to be small enough that it would be clear to everyone that victory came from God's strength. Give God the glory and honor for everything he does for you. Don't praise yourself or anyone else. Victory comes from God!

36

SAMSON'S CHOICES

What's Up

Samson was the strongest man who had ever lived. Since he had killed a few Philistines, they wanted very much to capture him. But he could always break free when he was tied up. So the Philistines made a deal with his girlfriend to find out why Samson was so strong. Even though he knew he shouldn't tell her his secret, he did. That was the beginning of the end for him. But, even though he was captured, Samson finished strong!

Action Adventure from Judges 16:4-30

Samson fell in love with Delilah. The rulers of the Philistines went to her and said, "Entice Samson to tell you what makes him so strong and how he can be overpowered. Then each of us will give you 1,100 pieces of silver."

So Delilah said to Samson, "Tell me what makes you so strong and what it would take to tie you up securely."

Samson replied, "If I were tied up with new bowstrings, I would become weak." The Philistines brought Delilah new bowstrings. She tied Samson up, and she cried out, "Samson! The Philistines have come to capture you!" But Samson snapped the bowstrings.

Delilah said, "You've been telling me lies!"

Samson replied, "If I were tied up with ropes that had never been used, I would become weak." So Delilah tied him up and cried out, "The Philistines have come!" But again Samson snapped the ropes.

Then Delilah said, "You've been making fun of me. Now tell me how you can be tied up."

Samson replied, "If you were to weave my hair into the fabric on your loom and tighten it, I would become weak." So while he slept, Delilah wove his hair into the fabric. Then she

Key Verse

People are counted as righteous, not because of their work, but because of their faith in God who forgives sinners.

Romans 4:5

tightened it. Again she cried out, "The Philistines!" But Samson yanked his hair away.

Then Delilah pouted, "How can you tell me, 'I love you,' when you don't share your secrets with me?"

Finally, Samson shared his secret. "My hair has never been cut. If my head were shaved, I would become as weak as anyone else."

Delilah lulled Samson to sleep and called in a man to shave off his hair. Then she cried out, "The Philistines!"

He thought, "I will shake myself free." He didn't realize the LORD had left him. The Philistines captured him. But before long, his hair began to grow back.

The people [said], "The one who killed so many of us is now in our power! Bring out Samson so he can amuse us!" So he was brought from the prison to amuse them.

If this is one of his lies, he is going to be really mad!

Samson said, "Place my hands against the pillars that hold up the temple." The temple was filled with Philistines, and there were about 3,000 on the roof. Samson put his hands on the pillars that held up the temple. Pushing against them, he prayed, "Let me die with the Philistines." And the temple crashed down. He killed more people when he died than he had during his lifetime.

Now What?

Samson trusted the wrong person. Delilah didn't love him. She just wanted the money the Philistines were going to pay her. So Samson gave up his secret, and his friendship with God was broken. But he prayed, and God forgave him, giving Samson another chance to defeat the Philistines. Never give up on yourself because you keep doing the wrong things or making bad choices. God will forgive you when you ask, just as he did Samson. God doesn't ever give up on you.

37

RUTH GAINS A FAMILY

What's Up

Naomi and her husband moved to Moab to escape the dry time when crops wouldn't grow in their country. But Naomi was left alone when her husband and both sons died. All she had left were two daughters-in-law. When Naomi returned to Bethlehem, one daughter-in-law, Ruth, chose to go with her. That choice changed Ruth's life, giving her an important role in the history of Jesus' family on earth.

Action Adventure from Ruth 1:1-9, 14-22; 2:1-3, 8-9, 17; 4:3-6, 11-17

A man from Bethlehem went to live in Moab, taking his wife and two sons with him. The man was Elimelech, and his wife was Naomi. Then Elimelech died, and Naomi was left with her two sons. The sons married Moabite women, Orpah and Ruth. Later, both [sons] died. So Naomi and her daughters-in-law got ready to leave Moab to return to her homeland.

Key Verse

Don't ask me to leave you and turn back. Wherever you go, I will go; wherever you live, I will live. Your people will be my people, and your God will be my God.

Ruth 1:16

On the way, Naomi said to her daughters-in-law, "Go back to your homes. May the LORD bless you."

Orpah kissed her mother-in-law good-bye. But Ruth replied, "Don't ask me to leave you. Wherever you go, I will go; wherever you live, I will live. Your people will be my people, and your God will be my God." When Naomi saw that Ruth was determined to go with her, she said nothing more. So Naomi returned from Moab, accompanied by her daughter-in-law Ruth. They arrived in Bethlehem at the beginning of the barley harvest.

There was a wealthy man in Bethlehem named Boaz, who was a relative of Naomi's husband.

One day Ruth said to Naomi, "Let me go out into the fields to pick up the grain left behind by anyone who is kind enough to let me do it."

Naomi replied, "Go ahead." So Ruth went out to gather grain, and she found herself working in a field that belonged to Boaz.

Boaz said to Ruth, "Stay right behind the young women working in my field. When you are thirsty, help yourself to the water they have drawn from the well." So Ruth gathered barley there all day.

Boaz said to the family redeemer, "Naomi is selling the land that belonged to Elimelech. If you want the land, then buy it in the presence of these witnesses. But if you don't want it, let me know, because I am next in line. Purchase of the land also requires that you marry Ruth, the Moabite widow. That way she can have children who will carry on her husband's name."

The family redeemer replied, "You redeem the land; I cannot

This turned out better than we could have hoped.

do it." Then the elders replied, "We are witnesses! May the LORD give you descendants by this young woman."

So Ruth became [Boaz's] wife. The LORD enabled her to become pregnant, and she gave birth to a son. The neighbor women said, "Now at last Naomi has a son again!" And they named him Obed. He became the father of Jesse and the grandfather of David.

Now What?

Ruth was a loyal daughter-in-law—kind and faithful. She traveled with Naomi to Bethlehem and took care of her when they got there. Loyalty is very important in families and in friendships. Loyalty means not walking away from someone just because you have an argument. Loyalty means giving a friend the benefit of the doubt when she hurts your feelings. Loyalty means standing up for a friend or family member when someone says something mean about him. Loyalty is a wonderful quality. If you have a loyal friend, thank that person for it.

38

A VOICE IN THE NIGHT

What's Up

Samuel was a young boy who lived in the Tabernacle, the tent where God's people worshiped him. Samuel helped the priest, Eli. However, one night Samuel had a most unusual experience. God spoke to him. At first Samuel wasn't sure what was happening, but Eli finally understood that God was speaking. God gave Samuel a message to pass along to the priest.

Action Adventure from 1 Samuel 3:1-20

Samuel served the LORD by assisting Eli. Now in those days messages from the LORD were very rare, and visions were quite uncommon. One night Eli, who was almost blind, had gone to bed. Samuel was sleeping in the Tabernacle near the Ark of God. Suddenly the LORD called out, "Samuel!"

"Yes?" Samuel replied. "What is it?" He got up and ran to Eli. "Here I am. Did you call me?"

"I didn't call you," Eli replied. "Go back to bed." So he did.

Key Verse

The LORD came and called as before, "Samuel! Samuel!" And Samuel replied, "Speak, your servant is listening."

1 Samuel 3:10

Then the LORD called out again, "Samuel!"

Again Samuel got up and went to Eli. "Here I am. Did you call me?"

"I didn't call you, my son," Eli said. "Go back to bed."

The LORD called a third time, and once more Samuel got up and went to Eli. "Here I am. Did you call me?"

Then Eli realized it was the LORD who was calling the boy. So he said, "Go and lie down again, and if someone calls again, say, 'Speak, LORD, your servant is listening.'" So Samuel went back to bed.

The LORD called as before, "Samuel! Samuel!"

Samuel replied, "Speak, your servant is listening."

Then the LORD said to Samuel, "I am going to carry out all my threats against Eli and his family, from beginning to end. I have warned him that judgment is coming upon his family forever, because his sons are blaspheming God and he hasn't disciplined them. So I have vowed that the sins of Eli and his sons will never be forgiven by sacrifices or offerings."

Samuel stayed in bed until morning, then got up and opened the doors of the Tabernacle as usual. He was afraid to tell Eli what the LORD had said to him. But Eli called out to him, "Samuel, my son. What did the LORD say to you? Tell me everything. And may God strike you if you hide anything from me!"

Samuel told Eli everything. "It is the LORD's will," Eli replied. "Let him do what he thinks best."

This is one conversation I am not going to enjoy.

As Samuel grew up, the LORD was with him, and everything Samuel said proved to be reliable. All Israel knew that Samuel was a prophet of the LORD.

Now What?

God spoke to Samuel two times, but Samuel didn't know it was God who was speaking. Finally, after the third time, and following Eli's advice, Samuel just said, "I'm listening." Then God gave him a message. Listening to God is important. It's hard to listen sometimes, though, because life is so noisy. To listen to God you must be quiet, and you must spend time reading his Word. Sometimes he speaks to you through the words of the Bible. Sometimes he speaks through your thoughts and through your feelings. Be quiet and listen to God.

39

GOD SAYS NO TO SAUL

What's Up

Saul was God's choice to be king of Israel. But Saul stopped obeying God, so God rejected him—God decided to put someone else in the king's place. Saul tried to talk his way out of the problem. He claimed again and again that he had obeyed God. But what Saul obeyed was his idea of what God's directions were. That didn't work.

Action Adventure from 1 Samuel 15:1-26

One day Samuel said to Saul, "The LORD told me to anoint you as king of Israel. Now listen to this message from the LORD: I have decided to settle accounts with the nation of Amalek for opposing Israel when they came from Egypt. Go and completely destroy the entire Amalekite nation."

So Saul mobilized his army. There were 200,000 soldiers from Israel and 10,000 men from Judah. Saul and his army lay in wait in the valley. Then Saul captured Agag, the Amalekite king, but completely destroyed everyone else. Saul and his men spared Agag's life and kept the best of the sheep and goats, the cattle, the fat calves, and the lambs—everything that appealed to them. They destroyed only what was worthless or of poor quality.

Then the LORD said to Samuel, "I am sorry that I ever made Saul king, for he has not been loyal to me and has refused to obey my command." Samuel was so deeply moved when he heard this that he cried out to the LORD all night.

The next morning Samuel went to find Saul. When Samuel finally found him, Saul greeted him cheerfully. He said, "I have carried out the LORD's command!"

"Then what is all the bleating of sheep and goats and the lowing of cattle I hear?" Samuel demanded. "Listen to what the LORD told me last night!"

Key Verse

The LORD is more pleased when we do what is right and just than when we offer him sacrifices.

Proverbs 21:3

"What did he tell you?" Saul asked.

Samuel told him, "The LORD has anointed you king of Israel and sent you on a mission. Why haven't you obeyed the LORD? Why did you rush for the plunder and do what was evil in the LORD's sight?"

"But I did obey the LORD," Saul insisted. "I carried out the mission he gave me. I brought back King Agag, but I destroyed everyone else. My troops brought in the best of the sheep, goats, cattle, and plunder to sacrifice to God."

But Samuel replied, "What is more pleasing to the LORD: your burnt offerings and sacrifices or your obedience to his voice? Obedience is better than sacrifice, and submission is better than offering. Rebellion is as sinful as witchcraft. So because you have rejected the command of the LORD, he has rejected you as king."

It was really more of misunderstanding than a sin.

Saul admitted, "Yes, I have sinned. I have disobeyed your instructions and the LORD's command. But now, please forgive my sin and come back with me so that I may worship the LORD."

But Samuel replied, "I will not go back with you! Since you have rejected the LORD's command, he has rejected you as king of Israel."

Now What?

King Saul told Samuel that he had not really disobeyed God. Either Saul had fooled himself into thinking he was obeying or he thought he was so important that he could do anything he wanted. Whatever his thoughts were, he was wrong. When God gives directions, he expects people to obey, not to give excuses about why they didn't. What can you learn from Saul? When you disobey God, don't make excuses. Admit what you've done, tell God you're sorry (and mean it), ask God to forgive you, and learn from your mistake what not to do again.

40

A NEW KING IN TOWN

What's Up

God would no longer let Saul be king of Israel, because Saul had not obeyed God. So the nation needed a new king. God chose the man he wanted to place in that position, and he sent the prophet Samuel to anoint that young man. This meant oil would be poured over his head. It would show that he was set apart to serve God. Everyone was surprised at God's choice—even Samuel himself was a bit surprised. But God told Samuel how he made his choice.

Action Adventure from 1 Samuel 16:1-13

The LORD said to Samuel, "You have mourned long enough for Saul. I have rejected him as king of Israel, so fill your flask with olive oil and go to Bethlehem. Find a man named Jesse there. I have selected one of his sons to be my king."

But Samuel asked, "How can I do that? If Saul hears about it, he will kill me."

"Say that you have come to make a sacrifice to the LORD. Invite Jesse to the sacrifice, and I will show you which of his sons to anoint for me."

When he arrived at Bethlehem, the elders of the town came to meet him. "What's wrong?" they asked.

Samuel replied. "I have come to sacrifice to the LORD." Samuel performed the purification rite for Jesse and his sons and invited them to the sacrifice.

When they arrived, Samuel took one look at Eliab and thought, "Surely this is the LORD's anointed!"

But the LORD said, "Don't judge by his appearance, for I have rejected him. The LORD doesn't see things the way you see them. People judge by outward appearance, but the LORD looks at the heart."

Key Verse

The LORD doesn't see things the way you see them. People judge by outward appearance, but the LORD looks at the heart.

1 Samuel 16:7

Then Jesse told Abinadab to step forward. But Samuel said, "This is not the one the LORD has chosen." Next Jesse summoned Shimea, but Samuel said, "Neither is this the one the LORD has chosen." All seven of Jesse's sons were presented to Samuel. But Samuel said to Jesse, "The LORD has not chosen any of these." Then Samuel asked, "Are these all the sons you have?"

"There is still the youngest," Jesse replied. "But he's out in the fields watching the sheep and goats."

"Send for him," Samuel said. "We will not sit down to eat until he arrives."

So Jesse sent for him. He was dark and handsome, with

Surely, you must have another son.

beautiful eyes. And the LORD said, "This is the one; anoint him."

So as David stood there among his brothers, Samuel took the olive oil and anointed David with the oil. The Spirit of the LORD came powerfully upon David from that day on.

Now What?

Through the process of choosing a new king, Samuel learned a great lesson. God doesn't care so much about how handsome or muscular or tall a person might be. He doesn't even care about how smart or clever a person is. God cares about a person's heart—whether or not a person wants to know, serve, and obey God. So, even though people may put a lot of importance on appearance or style, pay more attention to your heart and be sure that what's most important to you is knowing, serving, and obeying God. That's what matters.

41

A GIANT PROBLEM

What's Up

King Saul's army was lined up to fight the Philistines—enemies of God's people. But one Philistine soldier had all of King Saul's soldiers running scared. Goliath was a nine-foot-tall giant who dared the Israelite army to fight him. When young David heard Goliath's dare, he offered to fight the giant. David wasn't afraid, because he knew God would help him.

Action Adventure from 1 Samuel 17:3-9, 16-24, 32-50

The Philistines and Israelites faced each other on opposite hills. Goliath, a Philistine, came out to face Israel. He was over nine feet tall! He wore a bronze helmet, and his bronze coat weighed 125 pounds. His spear was tipped with an iron spearhead that weighed 15 pounds. Goliath shouted to the Israelites. "Choose one man to fight me! If he kills me, we will be your slaves. But if I kill him, you will be our slaves!" For forty days, every morning and evening, [he] strutted in front of the Israelites.

One day Jesse said to David, "Take this bread to your brothers." David's brothers were with Saul and the army. David hurried to his brothers. As he was talking with them, Goliath came out. David heard him shout his usual taunt. The Israelite army began to run away in fright.

"Don't worry about this Philistine," David told Saul. "I'll fight him!"

Saul replied. "There's no way you can fight this Philistine! You're only a boy."

But David persisted. "When a lion or a bear steals a lamb from the flock, I go after it with a club. If the animal turns on me, I catch

🔑 Key Verse

In your strength I can crush an army; with my God I can scale any wall. God's way is perfect. All the LORD's promises prove true. He is a shield for all who look to him for protection.

2 Samuel 22:30-31

it and club it to death. I'll do it to this Philistine, too, for he has defied the armies of the living God! The LORD who rescued me from the lion and the bear will rescue me from this Philistine!"

"All right, go ahead," [Saul] said and gave David his own armor. David put it on, strapped the sword over it, and took a step or two. He had never worn such things before.

"I can't go in these," he protested. So David took them off. He picked up five smooth stones and put them into his shepherd's bag. Then, armed only with his shepherd's staff and sling, he started across the valley to fight the Philistine.

Goliath walked out, sneering at this boy. "Am I a dog that you come at me with a stick? Come here, and I'll give your flesh to the birds and wild animals!"

David replied to the Philistine, "You come to me with sword, spear, and javelin, but I come

I'm REALLY glad God is on my side!

to you in the name of the God whom you have defied. Today the LORD will conquer you. Everyone here will know that the LORD rescues his people, but not with sword and spear. This is the LORD's battle, and he will give you to us!" Taking out a stone, he hurled it with his sling and hit the Philistine in the forehead. Goliath stumbled and fell. So David triumphed over the Philistine with only a sling and a stone.

Now What?

Bigger is not always better. That's an important lesson from the story of David and Goliath. Sure, Goliath was bigger and stronger. Sure, Goliath had more battle experience. Sure, David was just a kid. Sure, David's only experience was being a shepherd. But what mattered was that David was fighting with God's strength and power because his heart was focused on God. That's the only reason he could defeat Goliath. Outer strength doesn't matter. Inner strength does matter.

42

A FRIEND IN NEED

What's Up

Jonathan was King Saul's son, so he should have become the next king. But God chose David to be the next king. Even so, Jonathan and David became very close friends. Jonathan agreed to help David find out if King Saul wanted to kill him. It broke Jonathan's heart to find out that his father did want David dead.

Action Adventure from 1 Samuel 20:3, 12-42

David said, "Your father knows about our friendship, so he has said to himself, 'I won't tell Jonathan—why should I hurt him?' But I swear to you that I am only a step away from death!"

Jonathan told David, "I will talk to my father. If he speaks favorably, I will let you know. But if he wants you killed, may the LORD strike me if I don't warn you so you can escape. And may you treat me with faithful love as long as I live. If I die,

🔑 Key Verse

There are "friends" who destroy each other, but a real friend sticks closer than a brother.

Proverbs 18:24

treat my family with love. Wait by the stone pile. I will shoot three arrows as though I were shooting at a target. Then I will send a boy to bring the arrows back. If you hear me tell him, 'They're on this side,' you will know all is well. But if I tell him, 'The arrows are still ahead of you,' it will mean you must leave immediately."

When the festival began, the king sat at his place with Jonathan opposite him. But David's place was empty. When David's place was empty again the next day, Saul asked Jonathan, "Why hasn't the son of Jesse been here for the meal yesterday or today?"

Jonathan replied, "David asked if he could go to Bethlehem for a family sacrifice."

Saul boiled with rage. "I know that you want him to be king in your place. As long as that son of Jesse is alive, you'll never be king. Get him so I can kill him!"

"But why should he be put to death?" Jonathan asked his father. "What has he done?" Saul hurled his spear at Jonathan, intending to kill him. So at last Jonathan realized that his father was really determined to kill David.

The next morning Jonathan went out into the field and took a boy with him to gather his arrows. "Start running," he told the boy, "so you can find the arrows as I shoot them." The boy ran, and Jonathan shot an arrow beyond him. When the boy had almost reached the arrow, Jonathan shouted, "The arrow is still ahead of you." Only Jonathan and David understood the signal.

I'm out of here!

David came out and bowed to Jonathan. Both of them were in tears as they embraced each other and said good-bye. At last Jonathan said, "Go in peace. The LORD is the witness of a bond between us and our children forever." David left, and Jonathan returned to the town.

Now What?

King Saul's problem was that David was famous for killing Goliath. David had become more popular with the people than King Saul. And God had chosen David to replace Saul as king. So, yes, Saul was trying to kill David. But Jonathan was a true friend to David. True friends are worth more than gold. Do you have a really good friend who will always tell you the truth? Good for you. Are you that kind of friend too? Be the kind of friend who is gentle and kind and who also can be trusted.

43

TEMPTATION AT EN-GEDI

What's Up

David ran away because King Saul was trying to kill him. A group of men traveled with him as soldiers. Some of them told him to kill King Saul when he got the chance, but David refused to do it. He believed it would be wrong to kill the man God had made king. But he let King Saul know that when he had the chance to kill him, he chose not to.

Action Adventure from 1 Samuel 24

Saul was told that David had gone into the wilderness of En-gedi. So Saul chose 3,000 troops and went to search for David. At the place where the road passes some sheepfolds, Saul went into a cave. David and his men were hiding farther back in that very cave!

"Now's your opportunity!" David's men whispered. "Today the LORD is telling you, 'I will put your enemy into your power.'" So David cut off a piece of the hem of Saul's robe. But David restrained his men and did not let them kill Saul.

After Saul left the cave, David came out and shouted, "My lord the king!" When Saul looked around, David bowed before him. "Why do you listen to the people who say I am trying to harm you? You can see it isn't true. For the LORD placed you at my mercy back there in the cave. My men told me to kill you, but I spared you. Look, I have in my hand a piece of the hem of your robe! I cut it off, but I didn't kill you. This proves that I am not

🔑 Key Verse

You are a better man than I am, for you have repaid me good for evil. Yes, you have been amazingly kind to me today, for when the LORD put me in a place where you could have killed me, you didn't do it. Who else would let his enemy get away when he had him in his power? May the LORD reward you well for the kindness you have shown me today.

1 Samuel 24:17-19

trying to harm you, even though you have been hunting for me to kill me.

"I will never harm you. May the LORD judge which of us is right and punish the guilty one. He will rescue me from your power!"

Saul called back, "Is that really you, David?" Then he began to cry and he said, "You are a better man than I am, for you have been kind to me today. Who else would let his enemy get away when he had him in his power? May the LORD reward you well for the kindness you have shown me today. And now I realize that you are surely going to be king. Swear to me by the LORD that when that

I wonder if I would have been that kind?

happens you will not kill my family and destroy my line of descendants!"

David promised this to Saul with an oath. Then Saul went home, but David and his men went back to their stronghold.

Now What?

David didn't try to get back at King Saul for the way the king had treated him. He didn't want to be guilty of killing the man God had made king even when it seemed that God had brought the king to him. Trying to get even never turns out well. When a friend or family member hurts you, do you want to get even or make peace? If in your heart you want to be a child of God, you will be able to forgive and make peace instead of getting even. It's not easy, but it's the right thing to do.

44

DAVID TAKES THE THRONE

What's Up

When King Saul would not obey God, David was chosen by God to be the next king. A few years passed before David actually took the throne. He was only 30 years old when he became king. Right away God began giving him success, helping him have victory over the enemies of Israel. Soon all nations knew that God was with King David.

Action Adventure from 2 Samuel 5:1-12, 17-25

All the tribes of Israel went to David and told him, "In the past, when Saul was our king, you were the one who really led Israel. And the LORD told you, 'You will be the shepherd of my people Israel.'"

So King David made a covenant before the LORD with all the elders of Israel. And they anointed him king of Israel. David was thirty years old when he began to reign, and he reigned forty years in all.

Key Verse

David became more and more powerful, because the LORD God of Heaven's Armies was with him.

2 Samuel 5:10

David then led his men to Jerusalem to fight against the Jebusites, who taunted David, saying, "You'll never get in here! Even the blind and lame could keep you out!" But David captured the fortress of Zion, which is now called the City of David.

On the day of the attack, David said to his troops, "I hate those Jebusites. Whoever attacks them should strike by going into the city through the water tunnel." David made the fortress his home, and he called it the City of David. David became more and more powerful, because the LORD God was with him.

King Hiram of Tyre sent messengers to David, along with cedar timber and carpenters and stonemasons, and they built David a palace. And David realized that the LORD had confirmed him as king over Israel and had blessed his kingdom for the sake of his people Israel.

When the Philistines heard that David had been anointed king of Israel, they mobilized all their forces to capture him. But David was told they were coming, so he went into the stronghold. The Philistines arrived and spread out across the valley. So David asked the LORD, "Should I go out to fight the Philistines? Will you hand them over to me?"

The LORD replied to David, "Yes, go ahead. I will certainly hand them over to you." So David defeated the Philistines. "The LORD did it!" David exclaimed.

But after a while the Philistines returned. Again David asked the LORD what to do. "Do not attack them straight on," the

With the Lord on our side, we cannot lose.

LORD replied. "Instead, circle around behind and attack them near the poplar trees. When you hear a sound like marching feet in the tops of the poplar trees, that will be the signal that the LORD is moving ahead of you to strike down the Philistine army." So David did what the LORD commanded, and he struck down the Philistines.

Now What?

David did what Saul did not do—he obeyed God. When God told him just what to do, he did just what God said. Obeying every part of God's directions is very important. Obeying only some of what God tells us to do is as bad as not obeying at all. There is no way to sort of obey God but really just do what you want instead. God will not bless you for that. The only way to enjoy the good things God has for you is to obey all of his directions.

45

KINDNESS IN ACTION

What's Up

King Saul kept trying to kill David. But after Saul and his son Jonathan (David's friend) died in battle, David's first thought was to keep a promise he had made to Jonathan. He asked if anyone in Saul's family was still alive because he wanted to show kindness to them. One relative was still alive. He was Jonathan's son, Mephibosheth (meh-FIB-oh-sheth).

Action Adventure from 2 Samuel 9

One day David asked, "Is anyone in Saul's family still alive—anyone to whom I can show kindness for Jonathan's sake?" He summoned a man named Ziba, who had been one of Saul's servants. "Are you Ziba?" the king asked.

"Yes sir, I am," Ziba replied.

The king then asked him, "Is anyone still alive from Saul's family? If so, I want to show God's kindness to them."

Ziba replied, "Yes, one of Jonathan's sons is still alive. He is crippled in both feet."

"Where is he?" the king asked.

"In Lo-debar," Ziba told him, "at the home of Makir." So David sent for him and brought him from Makir's home. His name was Mephibosheth; he was Jonathan's son and Saul's grandson. When he came to David, he bowed low to the ground in deep respect.

David said, "Greetings, Mephibosheth."

Mephibosheth replied, "I am your servant."

"Don't be afraid!" David said. "I intend to show kindness to you because of my promise to your father, Jonathan. I will give you all the property that once belonged to your grandfather Saul, and you will eat here with me at the king's table!"

Mephibosheth bowed respectfully and exclaimed, "Who

🔑 Key Verse

Never let loyalty and kindness leave you! Tie them around your neck as a reminder. Write them deep within your heart.

Proverbs 3:3

is your servant, that you should show such kindness to a dead dog like me?"

Then the king summoned Saul's servant Ziba and said, "I have given your master's grandson everything that belonged to Saul and his family. You and your sons and servants are to farm the land for him to produce food. But Mephibosheth, your master's grandson, will eat here at my table." (Ziba had fifteen sons and twenty servants.)

Ziba replied, "Yes, my lord the king; I am your servant, and I will do all that you have commanded." And from that time on, Mephibosheth ate regularly at David's table, like one of the king's own sons.

You know, your dad was my best friend.

Mephibosheth had a young son. From then on, all the members of Ziba's household were Mephibosheth's servants. And Mephibosheth, who was crippled in both feet, lived in Jerusalem and ate regularly at the king's table.

Now What?

David was once called "a man after God's own heart." So it isn't surprising that he made the effort to find members of Saul's family so he could be kind to them. He was keeping a promise to his best friend, Jonathan, when he showed kindness to Jonathan's family. Being someone who keeps promises is an important quality in a friend. Doesn't it make you feel good when someone keeps a promise to you? Do you keep your promises? Do you tell your friends how thankful you are when they keep their promises to you? Promise keepers can be trusted.

46

A WISE DECISION

What's Up

David's son, Solomon, became king after his father. God offered to give Solomon whatever he asked for. He could have asked God to make him famous or wealthy, but he didn't. Solomon asked for wisdom to rule the people. God gladly gave him wisdom, and God also made him famous and wealthy. It wasn't long before Solomon was able to use that wisdom to help his people.

Action Adventure from 1 Kings 3:3-28

Solomon loved the LORD and offered sacrifices at places of worship. The most important of these places was at Gibeon, so the king sacrificed 1,000 burnt offerings there. That night the LORD appeared to Solomon in a dream and said, "What do you want? Ask, and I will give it to you!"

Solomon replied, "You have made me king but I am like a little child who doesn't know his way around. Give me an understanding heart so that I can govern your people well and know the difference between right and wrong."

God replied, "Because you have asked for wisdom and have not asked for a long life or wealth—I will give you what you asked for! I will give you a wise and understanding heart! I will also give you what you did not ask for—riches and fame!"

Later two [women] came to the king to have an argument settled. One began, "This woman and I live in the same house. I gave birth to a baby. Three days later this woman also

Key Verse

Because you have asked for wisdom in governing my people with justice and have not asked for a long life or wealth or the death of your enemies—I will give you what you asked for! . . . And I will also give you what you did not ask for—riches and fame!

1 Kings 3:11-13

had a baby. But her baby died when she rolled over on it. Then she got up in the night and took my son while I was asleep. She laid her dead child in my arms and took mine to sleep beside her. In the morning when I tried to nurse my son, he was dead! But when I looked more closely I saw that it wasn't my son at all."

The other woman interrupted, "It certainly was your son, and the living child is mine."

"No," the first woman said, "the living child is mine, and the dead one is yours."

Then the king said, "Both of you claim the living child is yours. Bring me a sword. Cut the living child in two, and give half to one woman and half to the other!"

The woman who was the real mother cried out, "Oh no! Give her the child—please do not kill him!"

Pretty clever, if I do say so myself.

But the other woman said, "All right, he will be neither yours nor mine; divide him between us!"

Then the king said, "Do not kill the child, but give him to the woman who wants him to live, for she is his mother!"

When Israel heard the king's decision, the people were in awe of the king, for they saw the wisdom God had given him.

Now What?

God's offer to Solomon was amazing—he would give him whatever he asked for. What would you have asked for? Riches? Fame? Power? Solomon showed that he already had some wisdom when he asked for wisdom to rule the people. Then he used that wisdom well, and we're still talking about it all these years later. Wisdom is more important than any of the other things that people think are important. You can gain wisdom by reading and studying God's Word and by asking him for it.

47

BUILDING GOD'S HOUSE

What's Up

God gave King Solomon the pleasure of building God's house, the Temple. Solomon took his job very seriously. He built a beautiful building, filled with fine wood and gold. It was a special home for the most holy God! God was there. He filled the Temple, and his people worshiped him there.

Action Adventure from 1 Kings 6:1-9, 15-21, 29-30, 38; 8:1-15

During the fourth year of Solomon's reign, he began to construct the Temple of the LORD. This was 480 years after the people of Israel were rescued from their slavery in Egypt. He built rooms against the outer walls of the Temple, all the way around the sides and rear of the building. The rooms were connected to the walls of the Temple by beams resting on ledges built out from the wall. The stones used in the construction of the Temple were finished at the quarry, so there was no sound of hammer, ax, or any other iron tool at the building site. After completing the Temple structure, Solomon put in a ceiling made of cedar beams and planks. The entire inside, from floor to ceiling, was paneled with wood, and the paneling was decorated with carvings of gourds and open flowers. Solomon overlaid the Temple's interior with solid gold, and he made gold chains to protect the entrance to the Most Holy Place. He decorated all the walls of the inner sanctuary and the main room with carvings of cherubim, palm trees, and open flowers. He overlaid the floor in both rooms with gold.

It took seven years to build the Temple.

Solomon then summoned to Jerusalem the elders of Israel and all the leaders of the

Key Verse

I have built this Temple to honor the name of the LORD, the God of Israel.

1 Kings 8:20

families. They were to bring the Ark of the LORD's Covenant to the Temple from its location in the City of David. The priests and Levites brought up the Ark along with the special tent and all the sacred items that had been in it. The priests carried the Ark into the inner sanctuary of the Temple—the Most Holy Place—and placed it beneath the wings of the cherubim. The cherubim spread their wings over the Ark.

Things are really getting serious now.

When the priests came out of the Holy Place, a thick cloud filled the Temple of the LORD. The priests could not continue their service because of the cloud, for the glorious presence of the LORD filled the Temple.

Then Solomon prayed, "O LORD, I have built a glorious Temple for you, a place where you can live forever!"

The king turned to Israel and gave this blessing: "Praise the LORD, the God of Israel, who has kept the promise he made to my father, David."

Now What?

Solomon built a beautiful building for God to live in. But Solomon didn't want to be praised for working hard on the building. He wanted to praise and honor God for his power, strength, love, and glory. He wanted the building to be just right for the most holy God. Now, since Jesus died and rose again and the Holy Spirit lives in us, our bodies have become the temple of God. He lives in your heart. Is your heart a special place for the most holy God? Do you keep your heart pure, and do you, in your heart, want to love and serve God more than anything else?

48

CONTEST ON MOUNT CARMEL

What's Up

Elijah was God's prophet. Sometimes he felt as if he was the only one left who served God. He challenged the prophets of the false god Baal to a contest. Elijah wanted everyone, including the king, to know who the true God is and to see his power. The people would see God's reply to Elijah's request. They would know that God heard Elijah's prayer when they saw how he answered!

Action Adventure from 1 Kings 18:22-39

Elijah said, "I am the only prophet of the LORD who is left, but Baal has 450 prophets. Bring two bulls. The prophets of Baal may choose whichever one they wish and cut it into pieces and lay it on the wood of their altar, but without setting fire to it. I will prepare the other bull and lay it on the altar, but not set fire to it. Then call on the name of your god, and I will call on the name of the LORD. The god who

answers by setting fire to the wood is the true God!"

Elijah said to the prophets of Baal, "You go first. Choose one of the bulls, and prepare it and call on your god. But do not set fire to the wood."

So they prepared one of the bulls and placed it on the altar. Then they called on the name of Baal from morning until noontime, shouting, "O Baal, answer us!" But there was no reply of any kind. Then they danced around the altar they had made.

About noontime Elijah began mocking them. "You'll have to shout louder," he scoffed. "Perhaps he is daydreaming. Or maybe he is away on a trip, or is asleep and needs to be wakened!"

Key Verse

When all the people saw it, they fell face down on the ground and cried out, "The LORD—he is God! Yes, the LORD is God!"

1 Kings 18:39

So they shouted louder. They raved all afternoon until the time of the evening sacrifice, but still there was no sound, no reply.

Then Elijah called to the people, "Come over here!" He repaired the altar of the LORD. Then he dug a trench around the altar large enough to hold about three gallons. He piled wood on the altar, cut the bull into pieces, and laid the pieces on the wood. Then he said, "Fill four large jars with water, and pour the water over the offering and the wood."

After they had done this, he said, "Do the same thing again!" And when they were finished, he said, "Now do it a third time!" So they did, and the water ran around the altar and filled the trench.

Elijah prayed, "O LORD, God of Abraham, Isaac, and Jacob, prove today that you are God

This is going to be a real problem!

in Israel. O LORD, answer me so these people will know that you are God." Immediately fire flashed down from heaven and burned up the bull, the wood, the stones, and the dust. It even licked up all the water in the trench! And when all the people saw it, they fell face down on the ground and cried out, "The LORD —he is God!"

Now What?

Elijah was brave. He stood alone against the king and all the prophets of Baal. Except, he wasn't really alone, because God stood with him.
God showed his power in his reply to Elijah in front of the prophets of Baal. There will always be people who think someone or something is more important or more powerful than God. But remember the story of Elijah, and stand strong for God. He hears your prayers and will answer by showing his strength and power!

49

A GENERAL'S PLEA

What's Up

Naaman was a commander in the army of Aram. That army had conquered the Israelites and taken many of them to be their slaves. One little Israelite girl became a servant for Naaman's wife. When Naaman developed the terrible skin illness of leprosy, this little girl played an important role. She suggested that Naaman see God's prophet, Elisha. She believed God would work through Elisha to heal him. Naaman listened to the wise little slave girl.

Action Adventure from 2 Kings 5:1-19

The king of Aram had great admiration for Naaman, the commander of his army. But Naaman suffered from leprosy. Aramean raiders had invaded Israel, and among their captives was a young girl who had been given to Naaman's wife as a maid. One day the girl said, "I wish my master would go to the prophet in Samaria. He would heal his leprosy."

Naaman told the king what the young girl said. "Visit the prophet," the king of Aram told him. "I will send a letter of introduction to the king of Israel."

When the king of Israel read the letter, he tore his clothes in dismay and said, "This man sends me a leper to heal! Am I God, that I can give life and take it away?"

Elisha heard that the king of Israel had torn his clothes in dismay. He sent this message to him: "Send Naaman to me."

Naaman waited at Elisha's house. But Elisha sent a messenger out to him: "Go and wash seven times in the Jordan River. Then your skin will be restored, and you will be healed of your leprosy."

Naaman became angry and stalked away. "I thought he would come out to meet me!" he said. "I expected him to wave

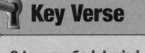

Key Verse

O LORD my God, I cried to you for help, and you restored my health.

Psalm 30:2

his hand over the leprosy and call on his God and heal me!" His officers said, "If the prophet had told you to do something difficult, wouldn't you have done it? So you should obey him when he says simply, 'Wash and be cured!'"

So Naaman went to the Jordan River and dipped himself seven times, as the man of God had instructed. His skin became as healthy as the skin of a young child, and he was healed! Then Naaman went to find the man of God and said, "Now I know that there is no God in all the world except in Israel."

Then Naaman said, "Please allow me to load my mules with earth from this place, and I will take it back home with me. From now on I will never offer burnt offerings or sacrifices to

This has to be the one, true God!

any other god except the LORD. However, may the LORD pardon me in this one thing: When my master the king goes into the temple of the god Rimmon to worship there and leans on my arm, may the LORD pardon me when I bow, too."

"Go in peace," Elisha said. So Naaman started home again.

Now What?

Naaman thought he was pretty special, didn't he? He thought he was so important that Elisha should come and speak to him personally. However, once he did the simple task Elisha told him to do, God healed him. We are always excited to see or read about the wonderful miracles God does. But sometimes God shows his amazing power through everyday blessings. Look for God's power everywhere—when you see a bird fly by or when you pray and your mom's back feels better, for example—and you will learn to trust God more and more!

50

ATHALIAH ATTACKS

What's Up

Athaliah (ahth-uh-LIE-uh) was one angry woman. After her son, King Ahaziah (ay-huz-EYE-uh), was killed, she acted like a crazy person, killing the rest of the family. The king's sister managed to grab the king's baby son, Joash, and save him from his grandmother's wild anger. The little boy was hidden and kept safe until he could be crowned king. He was still a young boy when he became king.

Action Adventure from 2 Kings 11

When Athaliah, the mother of King Ahaziah, learned that her son was dead, she began to destroy the rest of the royal family. But Ahaziah's sister took Ahaziah's infant son, Joash, away from the rest of the king's children, who were about to be killed. She put Joash in a bedroom to hide him from Athaliah. Joash remained hidden in the Temple of the LORD for six years while Athaliah ruled over the land.

In the seventh year of Athaliah's reign, Jehoiada the priest summoned the commanders and the palace guards to come to the Temple. He showed them the king's son. Jehoiada told them, "A third of you are to guard the royal palace. Another third are to guard the Sur Gate. The final third must stand guard behind the palace guard. Form a bodyguard around the king. Kill anyone who tries to break through. Stay with the king wherever he goes."

The commanders took charge of the men. They brought them all to Jehoiada, and he supplied them with the spears and shields that had once belonged to King David. The palace guards stationed themselves around the king, with their weapons ready. Then Jehoiada brought

Key Verse

He will cover you with his feathers. He will shelter you with his wings. His faithful promises are your armor and protection.

Psalm 91:4

out Joash, placed the crown on his head, and presented him with a copy of God's laws. They proclaimed him king, and everyone clapped and shouted, "Long live the king!"

When Athaliah heard all the noise, she hurried to the Temple. When she arrived, she saw the newly crowned king. The commanders and trumpeters were surrounding him, and people were rejoicing and blowing trumpets. When Athaliah saw this, she tore her clothes and shouted, "Treason!"

Then Jehoiada ordered, "Take her to the soldiers in front of the Temple, and kill anyone who tries to rescue her." They seized her and led her out to the gate where horses enter the palace grounds, and she was killed there.

Then Jehoiada made a covenant between the LORD and the king and the people

This can't be good!

that they would be the LORD's people. All the people went over to the temple of Baal and tore it down.

The commanders, the palace guards, and the people of the land escorted the king from the Temple of the LORD. The king took his seat on the royal throne. All the people of the land rejoiced, and the city was peaceful. Joash was seven years old when he became king.

Now What?

Do you sometimes wish you could do something for God now? Do you wonder if you will have to wait until you are grown up? The story of little Joash should make you feel pretty good then. You may never become a king or a queen, but everyone matters to God, young or old. Ask him what you can do for him right now. He will keep you safe and show you something kind or helpful you can do.

51

NEHEMIAH REBUILDS A WALL

What's Up

The wall around Jerusalem was crumbling and falling down. Nehemiah felt that this was a shame for God's city, so he decided to gather some men to rebuild the wall. But leaders of other nations were not happy about this project. They made fun of Nehemiah and then said they would attack the workers. But Nehemiah had a plan, and the workers listened to him.

Action Adventure from Nehemiah 4; 6:15-16

Sanballat was angry when he learned that we were rebuilding the wall. He mocked the Jews, saying, "What does this bunch of poor Jews think they're doing? Do they think they can build the wall in a single day? Do they think they can make something of stones from a rubbish heap?"

Then I prayed, "Hear us, God, for we are being mocked. May their scoffing fall back on their own heads, and may they themselves become captives in a foreign land! Do not blot out their sins, for they have provoked you to anger here in front of the builders."

At last the wall was completed to half its height around the entire city. When Sanballat heard that the gaps in the wall of Jerusalem were being repaired, he was furious and made plans to fight us. But we prayed and guarded the city day and night.

Then the people began to complain, "The workers are getting tired, and there is so much rubble to be moved. We will never be able to build the wall by ourselves."

Meanwhile, our enemies were saying, "We will swoop down and kill them and end their work." So

Key Verse

Two people are better off than one, for they can help each other succeed. If one person falls, the other can reach out and help. But someone who falls alone is in real trouble.

Ecclesiastes 4:9-10

I placed armed guards behind the lowest parts of the wall. I stationed the people to stand guard, armed with swords, spears, and bows. Then I called together the rest of the people and said, "Don't be afraid! Remember the Lord, who is great, and fight for your homes!"

When our enemies heard that we knew of their plans, we all returned to our work. But from then on, only half my men worked while the other half stood guard. The laborers carried on their work with one hand supporting their load and one hand holding a weapon. The trumpeter stayed to sound the alarm.

Then I explained, "We are separated from each other along the wall. When you hear the blast of the trumpet, rush to wherever it is sounding. Then our God will fight for us!" We worked from sunrise to sunset. I also told everyone living outside the walls to stay in Jerusalem. That way they and their servants

Nehemiah has a plan, and it includes all of us.

could help with guard duty at night and work during the day. During this time, none of us ever took off our clothes. We carried our weapons with us at all times, even when we went for water.

So the wall was finished—just fifty-two days after we had begun. When our enemies and the surrounding nations heard about it, they were frightened and humiliated. They realized this work had been done with the help of God.

Now What?

It helps to have a plan. Nehemiah knew that it would be good for each worker to be part of a team. By working together the workers would help one another get the work done. And they would help each other stay safe. Your family is a team that can work together. You and your friends might work together on projects at school and at church. And you are part of God's team, so be a good team member. Watch out for others, and help wherever you can!

52

ESTHER BECOMES QUEEN

What's Up

Esther won a beauty contest and became Queen of Persia. But Haman, an evil man in the kingdom, wanted all the Jewish people to be killed. These were God's people from the kingdom of Judah. Haman didn't know that Queen Esther was Jewish. She did not know yet that she had an important job to do.

Action Adventure from Esther 1; 2:2-10, 15-20; 3:1-12

King Xerxes gave a banquet for all the people in Susa. It was held in the courtyard of the palace garden. At the same time, Queen Vashti gave a banquet for the women. King Xerxes told [his servants] to bring Queen Vashti to him with the royal crown on her head. He wanted all the men to gaze on her beauty. But Queen Vashti refused to come. This made the king furious. He consulted with his advisers. "What penalty does the law provide for a queen who refuses to obey the king's orders?"

"Women everywhere will despise their husbands when they learn that Queen Vashti has refused to appear before the king. There will be no end to their anger. Issue a written law. It should order that Queen Vashti be banished and that the king should choose another queen more worthy than she," [his advisers said]. The king and his nobles thought this made good sense.

[The king's] personal attendants suggested, "Appoint agents to bring beautiful young women into the royal harem. Hegai will see that they are given beauty treatments. After that, the young woman who most pleases the king will be made queen."

A Jewish man whose name was Mordecai had a beautiful young cousin called Esther. When her father and mother died, Mordecai raised her as his own daughter. Esther was

Key Verse

A fool's proud talk becomes a rod that beats him, but the words of the wise keep them safe.

Proverbs 14:3

brought to the king's harem. Hegai was very impressed with Esther and treated her kindly. Esther had not told anyone of her nationality and family background, because Mordecai had directed her not to do so.

When it was Esther's turn to go to the king, he loved Esther more than any of the other young women. He declared her queen instead of Vashti. Esther continued to keep her family background and nationality a secret.

King Xerxes promoted Haman, making him the most powerful official in the empire. All the king's officials would bow down before Haman to show him respect whenever he passed by. But Mordecai refused to bow down or show him respect. Haman was filled with rage. He had learned of Mordecai's nationality, so he decided it was not enough to lay hands on

That was easier than I thought it would be!

Mordecai alone. He looked for a way to destroy all the Jews.

Haman approached King Xerxes and said, "There is a certain race of people scattered through your empire who refuse to obey the laws of the king. If it please the king, issue a decree that they be destroyed."

The king agreed, so a decree was written exactly as Haman dictated.

Now What?

Some people are just bad. Haman was so proud that he thought everyone should bow down to him. He couldn't stand it that Mordecai wouldn't do it. And it wasn't enough for Haman just to punish Mordecai—Haman wanted to get rid of all the Jews. Mordecai was not proud. He honored God and no one else. He would not give in even though Haman made it clear that Mordecai was risking danger. Two men—two ways to think about life. Which one would you want to be like?

53

BRAVE QUEEN ESTHER

What's Up

Queen Esther's cousin Mordecai knew that all of the Jewish people in the Persian Empire were in trouble. Haman had the king sign a law saying it was okay to murder all of them. So Mordecai asked Queen Esther to save her people—God's people, the Jews. The queen knew she would be risking her life going to the king without being called. The people prayed for her, and Mordecai reminded her that she might have become queen just for this time. So she took the chance.

Action Adventure from Esther 4–5; 7; 8:7-11

When Mordecai learned about all that had been done, he tore his clothes, crying with a loud wail. Queen Esther sent her attendant, [Hathach,] to find out what was troubling Mordecai. Mordecai gave Hathach a copy of the decree that called for the death of all Jews. He asked Esther to beg the king for mercy for her people.

Esther told Mordecai: "Anyone who appears before the king without being invited is doomed to die unless the king holds out his gold scepter."

Mordecai sent this reply: "Don't think that because you're in the palace you will escape when all other Jews are killed. Who knows if perhaps you were made queen for such a time as this?"

Esther sent this reply: "Gather the Jews and fast for me. Then I will go see the king. If I must die, I must die."

When [the king] saw Queen Esther, he held out the gold scepter. "What is your request? I will give it to you, even if it is half the kingdom!"

Esther replied, "Let the king and Haman come to a banquet I have prepared." So the king and Haman went to Esther's banquet.

Key Verse

Let's not get tired of doing what is good. At just the right time we will reap a harvest of blessing if we don't give up.

Galatians 6:9

The king said to Esther, "Now tell me what you want."

Esther replied, "Come with Haman tomorrow to the banquet I will prepare. Then I will explain."

Haman went home and bragged about the honors the king had given him. "Queen Esther invited only me and the king himself to a banquet. But this is worth nothing as long as I see Mordecai the Jew sitting at the palace gate."

Haman's wife suggested, "Set up a sharpened pole and impale Mordecai on it." This pleased Haman, and he ordered the pole set up.

The king and Haman went to Esther's banquet. The king said to Esther, "What is your request?"

Esther replied, "I ask that my life and the lives of my people be spared. Haman is our enemy."

Then one of the [servants]

I think he is going to get just what he deserves!

said, "Haman has set up a sharpened pole in his own courtyard. He intended to impale Mordecai."

"Then impale Haman on it!" the king ordered.

King Xerxes said, "Send a message to the Jews in the king's name." The king's decree gave the Jews in every city authority to unite to defend their lives.

Now What?

Mordecai said that Esther might have become queen for just such a time as when the Jewish people needed her. Esther listened to her cousin and did what she had to do to save her people. Wouldn't it be cool to know about a special job God has lined up for you at a certain time? You can know about that if you ask God to show you what he wants you to do. Then pay attention to the opportunities that come your way. Pay attention to the things you really feel like doing. That could be God directing you.

54

A JOB FOR ISAIAH

What's Up

The prophet Isaiah saw the glory of God and all the angelic beings who served him. Isaiah heard them tell one another how holy God is. This vision scared Isaiah. He was having this amazing dream while he was awake! He thought he would die because he saw God. But God had a job for Isaiah. The prophet was to give a message to the people that they should turn to God and worship him.

Action Adventure from Isaiah 6

It was in the year King Uzziah died that I saw the Lord. He was sitting on a throne, and the train of his robe filled the Temple. Attending him were mighty seraphim, each having six wings. With two wings they covered their faces, with two they covered their feet, and with two they flew. They were calling out to each other, "Holy, holy, holy is the LORD of Heaven's Armies! The whole earth is filled with his glory!"

Their voices shook the Temple to its foundations, and the entire building was filled with smoke.

Then I said, "It's all over! I am doomed, for I am a sinful man. I have filthy lips, and I live among a people with filthy lips. Yet I have seen the King, the LORD of Heaven's Armies."

Then one of the seraphim flew to me with a burning coal he had taken from the altar with a pair of tongs. He touched my lips with it and said, "See, this coal has touched your lips. Now your guilt is removed, and your sins are forgiven."

Then I heard the Lord asking, "Whom should I send as a messenger to this people? Who will go for us?"

I said, "Here I am. Send me."

And he said, "Yes, go, and say to this people, 'Listen carefully, but do not understand. Watch

Key Verse

I heard the Lord asking, "Whom should I send as a messenger to this people? Who will go for us?" I said, "Here I am. Send me."

Isaiah 6:8

closely, but learn nothing.' Harden the hearts of these people. Plug their ears and shut their eyes. That way, they will not see with their eyes, nor hear with their ears, nor understand with their hearts and turn to me for healing."

Then I said, "Lord, how long will this go on?"

And he replied, "Until their towns are empty, their houses are deserted, and the whole country is a wasteland; until the LORD has sent everyone away, and the entire land of Israel lies deserted. If even a tenth—a remnant—survive, it will be

Things are going to get worse before they get better!

invaded again and burned. But as a tree leaves a stump when it is cut down, so Israel's stump will be a holy seed."

Now What?

As soon as Isaiah's sins were forgiven, he was quick to say he was ready to do the work God wanted done. Of course, he had seen how holy God is, so he had a good understanding of God's power. But we know many more facts about God. We have the Bible and all the examples of the work God has done in the hearts and lives of his people. We should be even quicker to agree that we will help with God's work. Would you be as quick to say you are ready to work for God as Isaiah was? Are you eager to be God's servant and help others know about him?

55

A DESPERATE PRAYER

What's Up

God's people lived in the northern kingdom of Israel and the southern kingdom of Judah. King Sennacherib (sih-NACK-ur-ib) of Assyria was eager to defeat King Hezekiah (hez-ih-KI-uh) of Judah. So Sennacherib tried to destroy the people's faith in their king and in God himself. He liked to brag by saying that no king and no god could stand against Assyria. King Hezekiah prayed for God's rescue, and how do you think it came? Through a miracle!

Action Adventure from Isaiah 36:1-21; 37:1-7, 15-24, 29, 36-38

In the fourteenth year of King Hezekiah's reign, King Sennacherib of Assyria came to attack Judah. The king of Assyria sent his chief of staff to King Hezekiah with this message: "What are you trusting in that makes you so confident? Perhaps you will say, 'We are trusting in our God!' But with your tiny army, how can you think of challenging even the weakest of my master's troops?"

The chief of staff shouted in Hebrew to the people, "Hezekiah will never be able to rescue you. Don't let him fool you into trusting in the LORD. Make peace with [the king of Assyria]. Then you can continue eating from your own grapevine and fig tree and drinking from your own well. Have the gods of any other nations ever saved their people from the king of Assyria?"

The people were silent because Hezekiah had commanded, "Do not answer him."

King Hezekiah sent [messengers] to Isaiah, [saying,] "Today is a day of trouble, insults, and disgrace. But perhaps the

Key Verse

Keep on asking, and you will receive what you ask for. Keep on seeking, and you will find. Keep on knocking, and the door will be opened to you.

Matthew 7:7

LORD your God heard the chief of staff defy the living God and will punish him!"

The prophet replied, "This is what the LORD says: 'Do not be disturbed by this speech against me. The king will receive a message that he is needed at home. He will return to his land, where I will have him killed with a sword.'"

Hezekiah prayed: "You alone are God of all the earth. It is true that the kings of Assyria have destroyed nations. They have thrown the gods of these nations into the fire and burned them. But they were not gods at all—only idols of wood and stone. Rescue us from his power; then all the kingdoms of the earth will know that you alone are God."

Isaiah sent this message to Hezekiah: "Because you prayed about King Sennacherib, the LORD has spoken this word against him: By your messengers you have defied the Lord.

This isn't good!

Because of your raging against me and your arrogance, I will put my hook in your nose and my bit in your mouth. I will make you return by the same road on which you came."

That night the angel of the LORD went to the Assyrian camp and killed 185,000 Assyrian soldiers. Then King Sennacherib returned to his own land. One day while he was worshiping in the temple of his god, his sons killed him with their swords.

Now What?

Never forget the power of prayer. King Hezekiah could have given up when Sennacherib's chief of staff kept putting him down and making fun of God. Amazingly, Hezekiah and the people kept waiting for God to answer. When King Hezekiah prayed, God did answer. If you don't get a response to your prayers right away, do not give up. Keep praying and trusting, and wait to see what God has to say to you!

56

THE WORD IN THE FIRE

What's Up

When Jehoiakim (jeh-HOI-uh-kim) was the king of Judah, God told Jeremiah to write down his message for the people of Judah. God wanted them to stop sinning and start obeying him. When the message was read at the Temple, the people knew that the king needed to hear it too. As the message was read to the king, he tore off pages of it and threw it in the fire. That wasn't the end of God's message though!

Action Adventure from Jeremiah 36:1-10, 15-32

During the fourth year that Jehoiakim was king in Judah, the LORD gave this message to Jeremiah: "Get a scroll, and write down my messages against Judah, right up to the present time. Perhaps the people of Judah will repent."

So as Jeremiah dictated, Baruch wrote on a scroll. Then Jeremiah said, "Go to the Temple on the next day of fasting, and read this scroll. Perhaps they will turn from their evil ways and ask the LORD's forgiveness before it is too late."

People from all over Judah had come to the Temple that day. Baruch read Jeremiah's words. When [the officials] heard the messages, they looked at one another in alarm. "We must tell the king what we have heard," they said to Baruch. "But first, tell us how you got these messages. Did they come directly from Jeremiah?"

So Baruch explained, "Jeremiah dictated them, and I wrote them down in ink, word for word, on this scroll."

"You and Jeremiah should hide," the officials told Baruch. Then the officials left the scroll for safekeeping and went to tell the king what had happened.

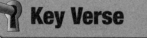

Key Verse

Repent of your sins and turn to God, so that your sins may be wiped away.

Acts 3:19

The king sent Jehudi to get the scroll. Jehudi read it to the king. The king was sitting in front of a fire to keep warm. Each time Jehudi finished reading three or four columns, the king took a knife and cut off that section of the scroll. He then threw it into the fire until the whole scroll was burned up. Neither the king nor his attendants showed any signs of fear or repentance. The king commanded his son to arrest Baruch and Jeremiah. But the LORD had hidden them.

After the king had burned the scroll, the LORD gave Jeremiah another message. "Get another scroll, and write everything again. Then say to the king, 'This is what the LORD says about King Jehoiakim of Judah: He will have no heirs to sit on the throne of David. His dead body will be thrown out to lie unburied. I will punish him and his family and

I am really not liking what I am hearing!

his attendants for their sins. I will pour out on them and on all the people of Jerusalem and Judah all the disasters I promised, for they would not listen to my warnings.'"

So Jeremiah dictated again to Baruch. He wrote everything that had been on the scroll King Jehoiakim had burned in the fire. Only this time he added much more!

Now What?

King Jehoiakim thought that by burning the scroll he was stopping God from calling the people to repent and to be sorry for their sin. The king was wrong. We will always have God's message. It's up to people to pay attention to it. God's message to the people then was the same as it is now—repent. Turn away from your sin. Have you done that? Have you told God that you are sorry for your sins? Have you asked his forgiveness? Are you obeying him now?

57

THREE MEN IN A FURNACE

What's Up

King Nebuchadnezzar (neb-you-kuhd-NEHZ-er) of Babylon had a huge golden statue made of himself. He commanded that all the people in the kingdom bow down and worship his statue every time they heard music. But three young Hebrew men refused to do that. They said they would not bow to anyone or anything except God. The king was so angry that he had the young men thrown into a blazing hot furnace. They trusted God to take care of them, and he did! God honored their faithfulness to him.

Action Adventure from Daniel 3

King Nebuchadnezzar made a gold statue ninety feet tall and nine feet wide and set it up in Babylon. A herald shouted, "When you hear the sound of musical instruments, bow to worship [the king's] gold statue. Anyone who refuses will be thrown into a blazing furnace."

Some astrologers went to the king and said, "Shadrach, Meshach, and Abednego,

Key Verse

Praise to the God of Shadrach, Meshach, and Abednego! He sent his angel to rescue his servants who trusted in him.

Daniel 3:28

whom you have put in charge of the province of Babylon, refuse to worship the gold statue."

Nebuchadnezzar flew into a rage and ordered that Shadrach, Meshach, and Abednego be brought before him. "Is it true that you refuse to worship the gold statue? I will give you one more chance to worship the statue. But if you refuse, you will be thrown into the blazing furnace. And then what god will be able to rescue you?"

Shadrach, Meshach, and Abednego replied, "If we are thrown into the blazing furnace, the God whom we serve is able to save us. But even if he doesn't, we will never worship the gold statue."

Nebuchadnezzar commanded that the furnace be heated seven times hotter than usual. Then he ordered men to tie them up and throw them into the furnace, fully dressed. Because the king had demanded such a hot fire, [it] killed the soldiers as they threw the men in. So Shadrach, Meshach, and Abednego, securely tied, fell into the flames.

Suddenly, Nebuchadnezzar jumped up in amazement and exclaimed, "Didn't we tie up three men and throw them into the furnace? I see four men walking around in the fire! And the fourth looks like a god!"

Nebuchadnezzar shouted: "Shadrach, Meshach, and Abednego, servants of the Most High God, come out!"

Shadrach, Meshach, and Abednego stepped out of the fire. Not a hair on their heads was singed, and their clothing was not scorched. They didn't even smell of smoke!

Then Nebuchadnezzar said, "Praise to the God of Shadrach, Meshach, and Abednego! He

I thought I said to put three men in the furnace!

sent his angel to rescue his servants who trusted in him. If any people speak a word against the God of Shadrach, Meshach, and Abednego, they will be torn limb from limb, and their houses will be turned into heaps of rubble. There is no other god who can rescue like this!" Then the king promoted Shadrach, Meshach, and Abednego to higher positions in the province of Babylon.

Now What?

It's pretty easy to be faithful to God when no one ever dares you to do something you believe is wrong. If everyone around you believes in God as you do, your faith in him is never questioned. But would you be as brave as the three young men were if you knew you would be punished for obeying God? The three young men showed that their hearts belonged completely to God. Nothing would scare them away from following him.

58

THE WRITING ON THE WALL

What's Up

Belshazzar (bell-SHAZ-zer) was now the king of Babylon, and he was celebrating! He threw a big party for the important people in his kingdom. But when a hand appeared and wrote a message on the wall of his palace, he began to panic. No one could tell him what the message said or what it meant. Then his mother remembered Daniel. God gave Daniel the wisdom to explain the message. But it wasn't good news for the king!

Action Adventure from Daniel 5

King Belshazzar gave a feast for 1,000 of his nobles. He gave orders to bring in the gold and silver cups that Nebuchadnezzar had taken from the Temple in Jerusalem. While they drank from them they praised their idols.

Suddenly, they saw a hand writing on the wall. The king saw the hand as it wrote, and his face turned pale. The king shouted for [the wise men of Babylon] to be brought before him. "Whoever can read this writing and tell me what it means will be dressed in purple robes of honor and will have a gold chain around his neck. He will become the third highest ruler in the kingdom!" But none of them could read the writing or tell him what it meant.

The queen mother said to Belshazzar, "There is a man in your kingdom who has within him the spirit of the holy gods. Daniel is filled with divine knowledge and understanding. He will tell you what the writing means."

So Daniel was brought in. The king asked him, "Are you Daniel? I have heard that you are filled with insight and wisdom. My wise men have tried to read the words on the wall and tell me their meaning, but they cannot do it. If you can read these words

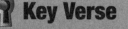

Key Verse

Honor the LORD for the glory of his name. Worship the LORD in the splendor of his holiness.

Psalm 29:2

and tell me their meaning, you will be clothed in purple robes of honor, and you will have a gold chain around your neck. You will become the third highest ruler in the kingdom."

Daniel answered, "The Most High God gave majesty, glory, and honor to Nebuchadnezzar. But when his heart and mind were puffed up, he was brought down from his throne. O Belshazzar, you knew this, yet you have not humbled yourself. You have had these cups from [the Lord's] Temple brought before you. You have been drinking wine from them while praising gods that neither see nor hear nor know anything at all. But you have not honored the God who gives you the breath of life!

"So God has sent this hand to write this message: MENE, MENE, TEKEL, and PARSIN. *Mene* means 'numbered'—God has

Now THAT is what I call making a statement!

numbered the days of your reign and has brought it to an end. *Tekel* means 'weighed'—you have been weighed on the balances and have not measured up. *Parsin* means 'divided'—your kingdom has been divided and given to the Medes and Persians."

That very night Belshazzar was killed. And Darius the Mede took over the kingdom.

King Belshazzar did not honor God, and God punished him for that. The king was proud and paid no attention to God. He didn't believe that the good things in his life and kingdom were from God. Do you honor God in your life? Do your words, actions, thoughts, and feelings show that you believe in God and that you are thankful for all he does for you?

Now What?

59

DANIEL IN THE LIONS' DEN

What's Up

Daniel had been a slave when he was first taken to Babylon, but he earned the respect of several kings because they saw how wise he was. When the Medes and Persians took over the kingdom, King Darius needed to choose leaders, and Daniel was at the top of the list. Some of the other leaders were jealous of Daniel and began looking for ways to get him in trouble. They did it by having the king make a law against praying to God. Daniel was punished. But God kept him safe for honoring him.

Action Adventure from Daniel 6:1-27

Darius the Mede decided to divide the kingdom into 120 provinces. Daniel proved himself more capable than all the other administrators. The king made plans to place him over the entire empire.

The other officers began searching for some fault in Daniel, but they couldn't find anything. They concluded, "Our only chance of accusing Daniel will be in connection with his religion."

The administrators and high officers went to the king and said, "Make a law that for thirty days any person who prays to anyone except you will be thrown into the den of lions. Sign this law so it cannot be changed." King Darius signed the law.

Daniel went home and knelt down with [his] windows open. He prayed three times a day, giving thanks to his God. The officials went to Daniel's house and found him praying. So they went straight to the king. "Did you sign a law that any person who prays to anyone except you, Your Majesty, will be thrown into the den of lions?"

"Yes," the king replied, "it is an official law of the Medes and Persians that cannot be revoked."

They told the king, "Daniel

🔑 Key Verse

I decree that everyone throughout my kingdom should tremble with fear before the God of Daniel. For he is the living God, and he will endure forever.

Daniel 6:26

still prays to his God three times a day."

The king tried to think of a way to save Daniel. In the evening the men went to the king and said, "According to the law of the Medes and the Persians, no law that the king signs can be changed."

So the king gave orders for Daniel to be thrown into the den of lions. The king said to him, "May your God, whom you serve so faithfully, rescue you." A stone was placed over the mouth of the den. Then the king returned to his palace. He couldn't sleep at all that night.

Early the next morning, the king hurried to the lions' den. He called, "Daniel! Was your God able to rescue you from the lions?"

Daniel answered, "My God sent his angel to shut the lions' mouths so that they would not hurt me. I have not wronged you, Your Majesty."

Nice kitty!

The king ordered that Daniel be lifted from the den. Then the king gave orders to arrest the men who had accused Daniel. He had them thrown into the lions' den.

King Darius sent this message to people throughout the world: "Tremble with fear before the God of Daniel. For he is the living God, and he will endure forever. He rescues and saves his people."

Now What?

Everyone knew that God had helped Daniel do some amazing things and that he was a man of good character. The men who wanted to get Daniel in trouble were pretty sure that Daniel would continue praying to God even though the new law said not to. God kept Daniel safe because Daniel had done nothing wrong. God honored Daniel because Daniel honored God. God's power to save Daniel from the lions was clear to everyone, and it is there for you, too!

60

A PROPHET WHO DIDN'T OBEY

What's Up

God had a job for Jonah to do. His job was very clear. He was to go to the city of Nineveh and preach about God. But Jonah didn't like the people of Nineveh. He didn't want them to turn away from evil and be saved. So he refused to go. God had an unusual way of getting Jonah's attention though. And he gave Jonah a second chance to obey.

Action Adventure from Jonah 1–2; 3:1-5, 10

The LORD gave this message to Jonah, "Go to Nineveh. Announce my judgment against it because I have seen how wicked its people are." But Jonah went in the opposite direction. He found a ship, bought a ticket, and went on board, hoping to escape from the LORD.

But the LORD hurled a powerful wind over the sea. Fearing for their lives, the sailors shouted to their gods for help. All this time Jonah was asleep. The captain shouted. "Get up and pray to your god! Maybe he will spare our lives."

The crew cast lots to see which of them had offended the gods and caused the terrible storm. When they did this, the lots identified Jonah as the culprit. "Why has this awful storm come down on us?" they demanded. "Who are you? What is your nationality?"

Jonah answered, "I am a Hebrew. I worship the God of heaven."

The sailors were terrified, for he had already told them he was running away from the LORD. They asked him, "What should we do to stop this storm?"

"Throw me into the sea," Jonah said, "and it will become calm again. This storm is all my fault."

The sailors cried out to

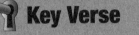

Key Verse

I cried out to the LORD in my great trouble, and he answered me.

Jonah 2:2

Jonah's God. "Don't make us die for this man's sin. And don't hold us responsible for his death." The sailors picked Jonah up and threw him into the sea and the storm stopped at once! The sailors were awestruck by the LORD's power.

The LORD arranged for a great fish to swallow Jonah. Jonah was inside the fish for three days and three nights. Jonah prayed from inside the fish, "I cried out to the LORD in my great trouble, and he answered me. O LORD, I sank beneath the waves. But you snatched me from the jaws of death. I will fulfill all my vows. For my salvation comes from the LORD alone." Then the LORD ordered the fish to spit Jonah out onto the beach.

The LORD spoke to Jonah a second time: "Go to Nineveh, and deliver the message I have given you." Jonah went. He shouted to the crowds: "Forty days from now Nineveh will be destroyed!" The people of Nineveh believed God's message. They put on burlap to show their sorrow. When God saw how they had put a stop to their evil ways, he changed his mind and did not carry out destruction.

Okay, already. I get it!

Now What?

The story of Jonah, the prophet who didn't obey, is important because it shows that God can teach you when you disobey and then help you to choose to obey next time. God gives second chances! Never give up on yourself just because you have sinned by disobeying God. He does not turn away from you. He waits for you to understand that you have disobeyed. Then he wants you to be sorry about what you did, change your mind, and come back to him. When you cry out to him, he will answer you. He will give you another chance and another and another . . . because he loves you.

61

THE NEW ELIJAH COMES

What's Up

Zechariah (zek-uh-RI-uh) was the priest chosen to go into the inner part of the Temple. There he would light the sweet-smelling incense for the offerings to God. It was an honor to be chosen to do this. While Zechariah was in there, an angel appeared to him. The angel said that Zechariah and his wife were going to have a baby. They were very old and had wanted to have children for a long time. This was going to be a special baby!

Action Adventure from Luke 1:5-23, 57-66, 80

There was a Jewish priest named Zechariah. His wife, Elizabeth, was also from the priestly line of Aaron. Zechariah and Elizabeth were careful to obey all of the Lord's commandments. They had no children because Elizabeth was unable to conceive, and they were both very old.

One day Zechariah was serving in the Temple. He was chosen by lot to enter the sanctuary and burn incense. A great crowd stood outside, praying.

Key Verse

From his abundance we have all received one gracious blessing after another.

John 1:16

While Zechariah was in the sanctuary, an angel of the Lord appeared to him. Zechariah was shaken with fear but the angel said, "Don't be afraid! God has heard your prayer. Your wife, Elizabeth, will give you a son, and you are to name him John. He will be great in the eyes of the Lord. He will be filled with the Holy Spirit, even before his birth. And he will turn many Israelites to their God. He will prepare people for the coming of the Lord."

Zechariah said, "How can I be sure this will happen? I'm an old man now, and my wife is also well along in years."

The angel said, "I am Gabriel! God sent me to bring you this good news! But since you didn't believe what I said, you will be unable to speak until the child is born."

Meanwhile, the people were waiting for Zechariah to come out, wondering why he was taking so long. When he finally did come out, he couldn't speak. Then they realized from his gestures that he must have seen a vision.

When Zechariah's week of service in the Temple was over, he returned home.

When it was time for Elizabeth's baby to be born, she gave birth to a son. And everyone rejoiced with her.

When the baby was eight days old, they all came for the circumcision ceremony. They wanted to name him Zechariah, after his father. But Elizabeth said, "No! His name is John!"

"What?" they exclaimed. "There is no one in your family by that name." So they used gestures to ask the baby's father what he wanted to name him. He motioned for a writing tablet, and to everyone's surprise he wrote, "His name is John." Instantly

There goes my peace and quiet.

Zechariah could speak again, and he began praising God.

Awe fell upon the whole neighborhood, and the news of what had happened spread throughout the Judean hills. Everyone asked, "What will this child turn out to be?" For the hand of the Lord was surely upon him in a special way. John grew up and became strong in spirit. And he lived in the wilderness until he began his public ministry.

Now What?

Zechariah had a visit from an angel. That meant the news he was getting was important. Since he didn't believe the news right away, God took his voice for a while. It's not a good thing to doubt God's message. Before long Zechariah and Elizabeth both believed God. And they were blessed with a baby boy. Believing God and obeying him result in blessing. Obeying every detail God gives is important!

62

THE BIRTH OF A SAVIOR

What's Up

God had promised long ago to send the Messiah to his people. The Messiah would be sent from God and would come to save the Jewish people. They had read about the Messiah for years. The angel Gabriel appeared to Mary and told this young girl that she would be the mother of the Messiah. That news must have been hard for her to believe. But she was ready to do whatever God wanted.

Action Adventure from Luke 1:26-38; 2:1-19

God sent the angel Gabriel to a virgin named Mary. She was engaged to be married to Joseph, a descendant of King David. Gabriel said, "Greetings, favored woman! The Lord is with you!" Confused, Mary tried to think what the angel could mean. "Don't be afraid, for you have found favor with God! You will give birth to a son, and you will name him Jesus. He will be very great and will be called the Son of the Most High. The Lord God will give him the throne of David. And he will reign over Israel forever; his Kingdom will never end!"

Mary asked the angel, "But how can this happen? I am a virgin."

The angel replied, "The Holy Spirit will come upon you. So the baby will be holy and will be called the Son of God. What's more, Elizabeth has become pregnant in her old age! For nothing is impossible with God."

Mary responded, "I am the Lord's servant. May everything you have said come true." Then the angel left her.

The Roman emperor, Augustus, decreed that a census should be taken throughout the Roman Empire. All returned to their ancestral towns for this census. Because Joseph was a descendant of King David, he

Key Verse

The Savior—yes, the Messiah, the Lord—has been born today in Bethlehem, the city of David!

Luke 2:11

had to go to Bethlehem, David's ancient home. He took with him Mary, his fiancée. And while they were there, the time came for her baby to be born. She gave birth to a son. She wrapped him snugly in strips of cloth and laid him in a manger, because there was no lodging available for them.

There were shepherds in the fields nearby, guarding their flocks of sheep. Suddenly, an angel of the Lord appeared and the Lord's glory surrounded them. They were terrified, but the angel reassured them. "Don't be afraid!" he said. "I bring you good news that will bring great joy to all people. The Savior—yes, the Messiah—has been born today in Bethlehem! And you will recognize him by this sign: You will find a baby wrapped snugly in strips of cloth, lying in a manger."

The angel was joined by the armies of heaven—praising God and saying, "Glory to God in heaven and peace on earth to

This must be BIG!

those with whom God is pleased."

When the angels had returned to heaven, the shepherds said, "Let's go to Bethlehem!" They hurried to the village and found Mary and Joseph, and there was the baby, lying in the manger. The shepherds told everyone what the angel had said about this child. All who heard the shepherds' story were astonished, but Mary kept all these things in her heart and thought about them often.

Mary was ready to serve God, even though she didn't understand how things could happen the way the angel told her. They did happen, and God's Son, Jesus, was born—a baby who would be the Savior of the world! God sent Jesus because he loves you and wants to be your friend. Have you asked Jesus to be your Savior? Do you know how very much God loves you?

Now What?

63

GIFTS FOR A KING

What's Up

When Jesus was born, a new star appeared in the eastern sky. Wise men who studied the sky knew that the star meant a new king had been born. They traveled for thousands of miles and followed the star to the house where Jesus lived with Mary and Joseph. The wise men's trip may have taken up to two years. When King Herod heard about the new king, he wanted to get rid of this king who would compete with his power.

Action Adventure from Matthew 2

Jesus was born in Bethlehem during the reign of King Herod. About that time some wise men from eastern lands arrived in Jerusalem, asking, "Where is the newborn king of the Jews? We saw his star as it rose, and we have come to worship him."

King Herod was deeply disturbed when he heard this. He called a meeting of the priests and teachers of religious law and asked, "Where is the Messiah supposed to be born?"

"In Bethlehem," they said. "The prophet wrote: 'And you, O Bethlehem in the land of Judah, a ruler will come from you who will be the shepherd for my people Israel.'"

Then Herod called for the wise men and learned the time when the star first appeared. He told them, "Go to Bethlehem and search for the child. When you find him, come back and tell me so that I can worship him, too!"

After this the wise men went their way. The star guided them to Bethlehem. It stopped over the place where the child was. They entered the house and saw the child with his mother, Mary, and they bowed down and worshiped him. Then they opened their treasure chests and gave him gifts of gold, frankincense, and myrrh. When it was time to leave, they

🔑 Key Verse

Where is the newborn king of the Jews? We saw his star as it rose, and we have come to worship him.

Matthew 2:2

returned to their own country by another route, for God had warned them in a dream not to return to Herod.

After the wise men were gone, an angel appeared to Joseph in a dream. "Get up! Flee to Egypt with the child and his mother," the angel said. "Stay there until I tell you to return, because Herod is going to search for the child to kill him." That night Joseph left for Egypt with the child and Mary, and they stayed there until Herod's death. This fulfilled what the Lord had spoken through the prophet: "I called my Son out of Egypt."

Herod was furious that the wise men had outwitted him. He sent soldiers to kill the boys in Bethlehem who were two years old and under. Herod's action fulfilled what God had spoken through the prophet: "A cry was heard in Ramah—weeping and great mourning."

Tell me about this dream again!

When Herod died, an angel appeared in a dream to Joseph in Egypt. "Take the child and his mother back to Israel, because those who were trying to kill the child are dead." So Joseph returned to Israel with Jesus and his mother. The family lived in a town called Nazareth. This fulfilled what the prophets had said: "He will be called a Nazarene."

Now What?

The wise men brought gifts to Jesus because they understood he was a special King sent by God. What kind of gift could you bring to Jesus? The wise men brought gold, frankincense, and myrrh—expensive and useful gifts. But do you know what gift Jesus would most like from you? He would most like your heart. That means your love, faithfulness, and worship are the most important gifts you can give him.

64

A LOST TWELVE-YEAR-OLD

What's Up

When Jesus was 12 years old, he went with his family to the Passover festival in Jerusalem. Many families walked together from their towns and villages to the big city. So Mary and Joseph didn't notice right away that Jesus wasn't with the group walking back home. When they realized he was missing, they rushed back to Jerusalem to look for him. What they found surprised them.

Action Adventure from Luke 2:41-52

Every year Jesus' parents went to Jerusalem for the Passover festival. When Jesus was twelve years old, they attended the festival as usual. After the celebration was over, they started home to Nazareth, but Jesus stayed behind in Jerusalem. His parents didn't miss him at first, because they assumed he was among the other travelers. But when he didn't show up that evening, they started looking for him among their relatives and friends.

When they couldn't find him, they went back to Jerusalem to search for him there. Three days later they finally discovered him in the Temple, sitting among the religious teachers, listening to them and asking questions. All who heard him were amazed at his understanding and his answers.

His parents didn't know what to think. "Son," his mother said to him, "why have you done this to us? Your father and I have been frantic, searching for you everywhere."

"But why did you need to search?" he asked. "Didn't you know that I must be in my Father's house?" But they didn't understand what he meant.

Then he returned to Nazareth with them and was obedient to

Key Verse

Jesus grew in wisdom and in stature and in favor with God and all the people.

Luke 2:52

them. And his mother stored all these things in her heart.

Jesus grew in wisdom and in stature and in favor with God and all the people.

I thought you would know where I would be.

Now What?

Jesus didn't just run off and get lost in Jerusalem. From the moment he could think, he knew that he was put on earth for a reason. What was always most important to Jesus was doing the work that God, his Father in heaven, had sent him to do. This story tells about the first time Jesus, God's Son, began speaking and teaching about God, the Father—and Jesus was only 12 years old! You have a reason for being on earth too. You are here to grow wiser and taller, and to learn about God so you can glorify God and honor him by the way you live.

65

JESUS' BAPTISM

What's Up

John the Baptist preached that people should repent of their sins and turn to God. When people did that, he baptized them in the Jordan River. But John knew that someone was coming after him who had even more authority to baptize—Jesus—God's own Son! John was shocked when Jesus came to him one day and wanted John to baptize him!

Action Adventure from Matthew 3

John the Baptist came to the Judean wilderness and began preaching. His message was, "Repent of your sins and turn to God, for the Kingdom of Heaven is near." The prophet Isaiah was speaking about John when he said, "He is a voice shouting in the wilderness, 'Prepare the way for the LORD's coming!'"

John's clothes were woven from coarse camel hair, and he wore a leather belt around his waist. He ate locusts and wild honey. People from all of Judea and all over the Jordan Valley went out to see and hear John. And when they confessed their sins, he baptized them in the Jordan River.

But when he saw many Pharisees and Sadducees coming to watch him baptize, he exclaimed, "Prove by the way you live that you have repented of your sins and turned to God. Don't just say to each other, 'We're safe, for we are descendants of Abraham.' That means nothing. Every tree that does not produce good fruit will be chopped down and thrown into the fire.

"I baptize with water those who repent of their sins and turn to God. But someone is coming soon who is greater than I am—

Key Verse

After his baptism, as Jesus came up out of the water, the heavens were opened and he saw the Spirit of God descending like a dove and settling on him. And a voice from heaven said, "This is my dearly loved Son, who brings me great joy."

Matthew 3:16-17

so much greater that I'm not worthy even to carry his sandals. He will baptize you with the Holy Spirit and with fire. He is ready to separate the chaff from the wheat. Then he will clean up the threshing area, gathering the wheat into his barn but burning the chaff with never-ending fire."

Then Jesus went from Galilee to the Jordan River to be baptized by John. But John tried to talk him out of it. "I am the one who needs to be baptized by you," he said, "so why are you coming to me?"

Jesus said, "It should be done, for we must carry out all that God requires." So John agreed to baptize him.

After his baptism, as Jesus

John says all the right things. He just looks kind of funny.

came up out of the water, the heavens were opened and he saw the Spirit of God descending like a dove and settling on him. And a voice from heaven said, "This is my dearly loved Son, who brings me great joy."

Now What?

Jesus paid attention to what had been written about himself, the Messiah. He obeyed what God the Father wanted him to do. We know that God was pleased with Jesus, his Son, because God told everyone about it who was present at the Baptism. God sent his Son to earth to do a job—to help people know how much God loved them. God wanted people to listen to all that his Son taught. How do you feel about Jesus? Do you believe that he is God's Son? Do you read and study his words so you will know how to do what pleases him?

66

JESUS IS TEMPTED AND HIS MINISTRY BEGINS

What's Up

The Spirit of God led Jesus out into the wilderness, away from everyone else. There the devil was allowed to tempt Jesus three different times. The devil tempted him to give up everything that showed he loved and trusted God the Father and would be faithful only to him. Jesus answered each of the devil's temptations with words from Scripture. Once the temptations were over, Jesus' work on earth began.

Action Adventure from Matthew 4

Jesus was led by the Spirit into the wilderness to be tempted by the devil. For forty days and forty nights he fasted and became very hungry. The devil said to him, "If you are the Son of God, tell these stones to become loaves of bread."

But Jesus told him, "No! The Scriptures say, 'People do not live by bread alone, but by every word that comes from the mouth of God.'"

Then the devil took him to Jerusalem, to the highest point of the Temple, and said, "If you are the Son of God, jump off! For the Scriptures say, 'He will order his angels to protect you. They will hold you up so you won't even hurt your foot on a stone.'"

Jesus responded, "The Scriptures also say, 'You must not test the LORD your God.'"

Next the devil took him to the peak of a high mountain and showed him all the kingdoms of the world. "I will give it all to you," he said, "if you will kneel down and worship me."

"Get out of here, Satan," Jesus told him. "For the Scriptures say, 'You must worship the LORD your God and serve only him.'"

Then the devil went away, and angels came and took care of Jesus.

Key Verse

The Scriptures say, "You must worship the LORD your God and serve only him."

Matthew 4:10

Jesus left Judea and returned to Galilee. This fulfilled what God said through the prophet Isaiah: "In Galilee, the people who sat in darkness have seen a great light. And for those who lived in the land where death casts its shadow, a light has shined."

From then on Jesus began to preach, "Repent of your sins and turn to God, for the Kingdom of Heaven is near."

One day as Jesus was walking along the shore of the Sea of Galilee, he saw two brothers—Simon, also called Peter, and Andrew—throwing a net into the water, for they fished for a living. Jesus called out to them, "Come, follow me, and I will show you how to fish for people!" They left their nets and followed him.

A little farther up the shore he saw two other brothers, James and John, sitting in a boat with their father, Zebedee, repairing

Good news travels fast.

their nets. He called them to come, too. They immediately followed him.

Jesus traveled throughout Galilee, teaching the Good News about the Kingdom. And he healed every kind of disease and illness. News about him spread, and people soon began bringing all who were sick. He healed them all. Large crowds followed him wherever he went.

Now What?

Jesus can identify with you when you want to do something that you know is wrong. He was tempted—after not eating for 40 days. He was tired, hungry, and weak. But he didn't give in to the devil's temptations. Jesus had God's Word hidden deep in his heart, and that's what kept him strong. If knowing God's Word was important for Jesus, it must be important for you, too. Read God's Word and memorize some of the verses. Then you will remember them when you need help to fight temptation.

67

WATER INTO WINE

What's Up

Jesus and some of his friends went to the wedding celebration of a friend. Jesus' mother happened to be there too. The host of the party ran out of wine. That was a serious problem. Mary, Jesus' mother, knew Jesus could help the host somehow. She told the servants to do whatever he told them. They did, and the result was Jesus' very first miracle. He was able to perform a miracle because, as the Son of God, he had the power of God within him.

Action Adventure from John 2:1-11

There was a wedding celebration in the village of Cana in Galilee. Jesus' mother was there, and Jesus and his disciples were also invited to the celebration. The wine supply ran out during the festivities, so Jesus' mother told him, "They have no more wine."

"Dear woman, that's not our problem," Jesus replied. "My time has not yet come."

But his mother told the servants, "Do whatever he tells you."

Standing nearby were six stone water jars, used for Jewish ceremonial washing. Each could hold twenty to thirty gallons. Jesus told the servants, "Fill the jars with water." When the jars had been filled, he said, "Now dip some out, and take it to the master of ceremonies." So the servants followed his instructions.

When the master of ceremonies tasted the water that was now wine, not knowing where it had come from (though, of course, the servants knew), he called the bridegroom over. "A host always serves the best wine first," he said. "Then, when everyone has had a lot to drink, he brings out the less

Key Verse

He does great things too marvelous to understand. He performs countless miracles.

Job 9:10

expensive wine. But you have kept the best until now!"

This miraculous sign at Cana in Galilee was the first time Jesus revealed his glory. And his disciples believed in him.

I don't want to be the one to take this to the master!

Now What?

Jesus' first miracle may not seem like a big deal. But the fact that Jesus did this miracle shows that he cares about the everyday problems you have. He's not concerned only about the big things that happen to you. He cares about every part of your life. How cool is that? Jesus, who has unlimited power and strength, is working for you every single day.

68

FISHING FOR DISCIPLES

What's Up

One day a huge crowd of people was moving in toward Jesus until he was nearly pushed into the Sea of Galilee. Jesus saw two boats on the shore, so he climbed into one of them to finish his message. Then he told the four fishermen to take their boats out into the water and fish. After filling both boats with fish, the men were ready to follow Jesus! Those four fishermen were Jesus' first followers—his first disciples.

Action Adventure from Luke 5:1-11

One day as Jesus was preaching on the shore of the Sea of Galilee, great crowds pressed in on him to listen to the word of God. He noticed two empty boats at the water's edge, for the fishermen had left them and were washing their nets. Stepping into one of the boats, Jesus asked Simon, its owner, to push it out into the water. So he sat in the boat and taught the crowds from there.

When he had finished speaking, he said to Simon, "Now go out where it is deeper, and let down your nets to catch some fish."

"Master," Simon replied, "we worked hard all last night and didn't catch a thing. But if you say so, I'll let the nets down again." And this time their nets were so full of fish they began to tear! A shout for help brought their partners in the other boat, and soon both boats were filled with fish and on the verge of sinking.

When Simon Peter realized what had happened, he fell to his knees before Jesus and said, "Oh, Lord, please leave me—I'm too much of a sinner to be around you." For he was awestruck by the number of fish they had caught, as were the others with him. His partners, James and John, the sons of Zebedee, were also amazed.

Key Verse

From now on you'll be fishing for people!

Luke 5:10

Jesus replied to Simon, "Don't be afraid! From now on you'll be fishing for people!" And as soon as they landed, they left everything and followed Jesus.

How can this be? We fished all night and didn't catch a thing!

Now What?

God doesn't need people to do his work on earth. He has the power, wisdom, and authority to do anything he wants to do. However, God chooses to give people the opportunity of working with him to spread the message of his love around the world. Jesus began this when he called his disciples to travel with him, learn from him, see his miracles, and continue his work. You can have the same opportunity if you read God's Word and pray to him so you get to know him better and better. Then you can fish for people and tell them what you're learning about God and his Son, Jesus!

69

HEALING AT THE POOL OF BETHESDA

What's Up

Jesus came to Jerusalem to celebrate one of the Jewish holy days. Crowds of sick people lay near the pool of Bethesda. Jesus went up to one man and asked if he would like to get into the water and be healed. But the man said he had no one to help him into the water. Jesus told the man to get up—he was healed! Some of the religious leaders became angry with Jesus and began looking for ways to get him into trouble.

Action Adventure from John 5:1-24

Jesus returned to Jerusalem for one of the Jewish holy days. Inside the city, near the Sheep Gate, was the pool of Bethesda, with five covered porches. Crowds of sick people lay on the porches. One of the men lying there had been sick for thirty-eight years. When Jesus saw him, he asked, "Would you like to get well?"

"I can't, sir," the sick man said. "I have no one to put me into the pool when the water bubbles up. Someone else always gets there ahead of me."

Jesus told him, "Stand up, pick up your mat, and walk!"

Instantly, the man was healed! He rolled up his sleeping mat and began walking! But this miracle happened on the Sabbath, so the Jewish leaders objected. They said to the man who was cured, "You can't work on the Sabbath! The law doesn't allow you to carry that sleeping mat!"

But he replied, "The man who healed me told me, 'Pick up your mat and walk.'"

"Who said such a thing as that?" they demanded.

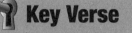

Key Verse

I tell you the truth, those who listen to my message and believe in God who sent me have eternal life. They will never be condemned for their sins, but they have already passed from death into life.

John 5:24

The man didn't know, for Jesus had disappeared into the crowd. But afterward Jesus found him in the Temple and told him, "Now you are well; so stop sinning." Then the man told the Jewish leaders that it was Jesus who healed him.

The Jewish leaders began harassing Jesus for breaking the Sabbath rules. But Jesus replied, "My Father is always working, and so am I." So the Jewish leaders tried harder to find a way to kill him. For he not only broke the Sabbath, he called God his Father, making himself equal with God.

So Jesus explained, "I tell you the truth, the Son can do nothing by himself. He does only what he sees the Father doing. For just as the Father

All I know is, I am HEALED!

gives life to those he raises from the dead, so the Son gives life to anyone he wants. Anyone who does not honor the Son is certainly not honoring the Father who sent him. I tell you the truth, those who listen to my message and believe in God who sent me have eternal life."

Now What?

Jesus showed his compassion—his loving care and understanding—for people who needed healing at the pool of Bethesda. He didn't care about the rules the religious leaders had made about healing on the Sabbath, the day of rest. He saw a need, and he took care of it. It is more important to listen to what God tells you to do than to listen to what people who are not loving say is right or wrong. Listen to God, follow him, and obey him. You will show respect for God, along with love and compassion for people, by doing that.

70

AMAZING FAITH

What's Up

A Roman officer sent some Jewish leaders to Jesus with an important request. The officer had a slave who was very sick—in fact, nearly dead. And the Roman believed that Jesus could heal the slave. This Roman officer had such amazing faith that he sent a message saying that Jesus didn't have to come to his home. He believed that Jesus could heal the slave just by saying it would be so. Jesus said he had never seen such great faith before.

Action Adventure from Luke 7:1-10

Jesus returned to Capernaum. At that time the highly valued slave of a Roman officer was sick and near death. When the officer heard about Jesus, he sent some respected Jewish elders to ask him to come and heal his slave. So they earnestly begged Jesus to help the man. "If anyone deserves your help, he does," they said, "for he loves the Jewish people and even built a synagogue for us."

Key Verse

Faith is the confidence that what we hope for will actually happen; it gives us assurance about things we cannot see.

Hebrews 11:1

So Jesus went with them. But just before they arrived at the house, the officer sent some friends to say, "Lord, don't trouble yourself by coming to my home, for I am not worthy of such an honor. I am not even worthy to come and meet you. Just say the word from where you are, and my servant will be healed. I know this because I am under the authority of my superior officers, and I have authority over my soldiers. I only need to say, 'Go,' and they go, or 'Come,' and they come. And if I say to my slaves, 'Do this,' they do it."

When Jesus heard this, he was amazed. Turning to the crowd that was following him, he said, "I tell you, I haven't seen faith like this in all Israel!"

And when the officer's friends returned to his house, they found the slave completely healed.

Now that is what I call FAITH!

Now What?

Anyone can say that he or she has faith in Jesus. Just saying words is easy, especially when things are going well and you don't think you need him much. But when you have a real problem and you must actually believe that Jesus is hearing your prayers and can do what you need for him to do, then the truth of your faith shows. The Roman officer knew that Jesus could just speak words and heal his slave. Do you trust Jesus that much? Do you believe he has the power and strength to take care of you completely, whatever the problems are that you might face today or tomorrow or the next day?

71

SENDING SPIRITS AWAY

What's Up

Jesus and his followers were climbing out of their boat when a man came out to meet Jesus. The man was controlled by evil spirits, also called demons. The demons started screaming at Jesus when he commanded them to come out of the man. Jesus sent the demons into a herd of pigs, and they jumped off a cliff. This made Jesus even more famous than he had been.

Action Adventure from Luke 8:26-39

They arrived in the region across the lake from Galilee. As Jesus was climbing out of the boat, a man who was possessed by demons came out to meet him. For a long time he had been homeless and naked, living in a cemetery outside the town.

As soon as he saw Jesus, he fell down in front of him. Then he screamed, "Why are you interfering with me, Jesus, Son of the Most High God? Please, I beg you, don't torture me!" For Jesus had already commanded the evil spirit to come out of him. This spirit had often taken control of the man. Even when he was placed under guard and put in chains, he simply broke them and rushed out into the wilderness, completely under the demon's power.

Jesus demanded, "What is your name?"

"Legion," he replied, for he was filled with many demons. The demons kept begging Jesus not to send them into the bottomless pit.

There happened to be a large herd of pigs feeding on the hillside nearby, and the demons begged him to let them enter into the pigs. So Jesus gave them permission. Then the demons came out of the man

🔑 Key Verse

God anointed Jesus of Nazareth with the Holy Spirit and with power. Then Jesus went around doing good and healing all who were oppressed by the devil, for God was with him.

Acts 10:38

and entered the pigs, and the entire herd plunged down the steep hillside into the lake and drowned.

When the herdsmen saw it, they fled to the nearby town, spreading the news as they ran. People rushed out to see what had happened. A crowd soon gathered around Jesus, and they saw the man who had been freed from the demons. He was sitting at Jesus' feet, fully clothed and perfectly sane, and they were all afraid.

Then those who had seen what happened told the others how the demon-possessed man had been healed. And all the people in the region begged Jesus to go away and leave them alone, for a great wave of fear swept over them.

Jesus returned to the boat and left, crossing back to the

I bet that isn't what those demons had in mind.

other side of the lake. The man who had been freed from the demons begged to go with him. But Jesus sent him home, saying, "No, go back to your family, and tell them everything God has done for you." So he went all through the town proclaiming the great things Jesus had done for him.

Now What?

Isn't it amazing that even the demons recognized who Jesus was? Every time Jesus performed a miracle, he became more famous. Then more people came to see him. When Jesus had sent the demons out of the man, he told the man to go home and tell people what God had done for him. That's a good lesson for us, too. When God does something for you—answers a prayer, for example—tell people. Give him credit! And tell others how thankful you are for what he did. That way more people will know about him and his power and love.

72

JESUS CALMS A STORM

What's Up

Jesus would teach large crowds of people about God all day long. One evening he told his disciples to get into their boat and cross the lake. That gave them a little time away from the crowds. As soon as Jesus got into the boat, he fell asleep. A big storm blew in, but he didn't even wake up. When his disciples woke him, they saw his amazing power again!

Action Adventure from Mark 4:35-41

As evening came, Jesus said to his disciples, "Let's cross to the other side of the lake." So they took Jesus in the boat and started out, leaving the crowds behind (although other boats followed). But soon a fierce storm came up. High waves were breaking into the boat, and it began to fill with water.

Jesus was sleeping at the back of the boat with his head on a cushion. The disciples woke him up, shouting, "Teacher, don't you care that we're going to drown?"

When Jesus woke up, he rebuked the wind and said to the waves, "Silence! Be still!" Suddenly the wind stopped, and there was a great calm. Then he asked them, "Why are you afraid? Do you still have no faith?"

The disciples were absolutely terrified. "Who is this man?" they asked each other. "Even the wind and waves obey him!"

Key Verse

Faith comes from hearing, that is, hearing the Good News about Christ.

Romans 10:17

He is no ordinary teacher!

Now What?

The disciples had spent a lot of time with Jesus. They had seen him do many miracles. They had heard him teaching people about God and about how to live. But, even with all that, they still didn't seem to understand that he was the Messiah—the one God had promised to send. Do you understand that Jesus is the Messiah, the Son of God? You have all the stories in the Bible to show you his power, strength, love, and care. You can see his work in your life, his answers to your prayers. Do these things make your faith strong?

73

New Life for a Girl and a Woman

What's Up

There was a large crowd around Jesus, as usual. One man came through the crowd to ask Jesus to help his daughter, who was very sick. Jairus was a leader in the synagogue, the local place of worship. And he believed Jesus could help his girl. But, before Jesus went home with Jairus, a woman who had been sick for 12 years reached through the crowd and touched Jesus' robe. She also believed in Jesus' power to heal.

Action Adventure from Mark 5:21-43

Jesus got into the boat and went back to the other side of the lake, where a large crowd gathered around him on the shore. Then a leader of the local synagogue, whose name was Jairus, arrived. When he saw Jesus, he fell at his feet, pleading with him. "My daughter is dying," he said. "Please come and heal her so she can live."

Jesus went with him, and all the people followed. A woman in the crowd had suffered a great deal from many doctors, and over the years she had spent everything she had to pay them but had gotten no better. She had heard about Jesus, so she came up behind him through the crowd and touched his robe. She thought, "If I can just touch his robe, I will be healed." Immediately she could feel in her body that she had been healed.

Jesus realized at once that healing power had gone out from him, so he turned around in the crowd and asked, "Who touched my robe?"

His disciples said to him, "Look at this crowd around you. How can you ask, 'Who touched me?'"

But he kept on looking around to see who had done it. The woman, trembling at the realization of what had happened

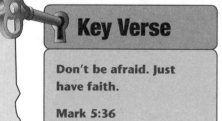

Key Verse

Don't be afraid. Just have faith.

Mark 5:36

to her, came to him and told him what she had done. He said to her, "Daughter, your faith has made you well. Go in peace."

While he was still speaking to her, messengers arrived from the home of Jairus, the leader of the synagogue. They told him, "Your daughter is dead. There's no use troubling the Teacher now."

But Jesus overheard them and said to Jairus, "Don't be afraid. Just have faith."

Then Jesus stopped the crowd and wouldn't let anyone go with him except Peter, James, and John (the brother of James). When they came to the home of the synagogue leader, Jesus saw much commotion and weeping. He went inside and asked, "Why all this commotion and weeping? The child isn't dead; she's only asleep."

The crowd laughed at him. But he made them all leave. He took

This is going to be good!

the girl's father and mother and his three disciples into the room where the girl was lying. Holding her hand, he said to her, "Little girl, get up!" And the girl, who was twelve years old, immediately stood up and walked! They were totally amazed. Jesus gave them strict orders not to tell anyone what had happened, and then he told them to give her something to eat.

Now What?

The woman who had been sick for a long time had so much faith that she believed just touching Jesus' robe would heal her. That's a strong faith. Then, when Jairus's daughter died, everyone in his house also got to see an amazing miracle from Jesus. If you were healed from an illness or saw a miracle like a dead person coming back to life, would you believe in Jesus? Would you tell others about his healing power and wonderful miracles? The Bible is full of true stories about Jesus' work.

74

FOOD FOR FIVE THOUSAND

What's Up

Once again crowds of people gathered to hear Jesus teach. Late in the afternoon, his disciples suggested that he send the people away so they could get food for dinner. But Jesus wanted the disciples to feed the people, even though they didn't have any food. One little boy agreed to give his lunch to Jesus. And after Jesus blessed that lunch, more than 5,000 people ate all they wanted from it.

Action Adventure from John 6:1-14

Jesus crossed over to the far side of the Sea of Galilee. A huge crowd kept following him wherever he went, because they saw his miraculous signs as he healed the sick. Then Jesus climbed a hill and sat down with his disciples around him. (It was nearly time for the Jewish Passover celebration.) Jesus soon saw a huge crowd of people coming to look for him. Turning to Philip, he asked, "Where can we buy bread to feed all these people?" He was testing Philip, for he already knew what he was going to do.

Philip replied, "Even if we worked for months, we wouldn't have enough money to feed them!"

Then Andrew, Simon Peter's brother, spoke up. "There's a young boy here with five barley loaves and two fish. But what good is that with this huge crowd?"

"Tell everyone to sit down," Jesus said. So they all sat down on the grassy slopes. (The men alone numbered about 5,000.) Then Jesus took the loaves, gave thanks to God, and distributed them to the people. Afterward he did the same with the fish. And they all ate as much

🔑 Key Verse

Look at the birds. They don't plant or harvest or store food in barns, for your heavenly Father feeds them. And aren't you far more valuable to him than they are?

Matthew 6:26

as they wanted. After everyone was full, Jesus told his disciples, "Now gather the leftovers, so that nothing is wasted." So they picked up the pieces and filled twelve baskets with scraps left by the people who had eaten from the five barley loaves.

When the people saw him do this miraculous sign, they exclaimed, "Surely, he is the Prophet we have been expecting!"

Where did all this food come from?

Now What?

Is it surprising to you to think that God cares about whether or not you're hungry? He cares about your day-in and day-out needs. Sometimes he even gives you what you want but don't really need. Stories like the feeding of the 5,000 show that Jesus cares about our physical needs, such as food, as well as spiritual needs, such as trusting God. He cares about all of your basic needs, so pray about them—not just for yourself, but also for those people around the world who need food and water just to survive. Show your care for those who are hungry, too, by giving and helping in whatever way you can.

75

WALKING ON WATER

What's Up

On the evening after Jesus fed over 5,000 people, he told his disciples to get into their boat. He wanted them to cross to the other side of the lake, while he went up into the hills by himself to pray. During the night a storm blew in on the lake, and the disciples were in big trouble. Jesus went to them—walking on top of the water. Peter was so amazed that he wanted to walk on the water too!

Action Adventure from Matthew 14:22-33

Jesus insisted that his disciples get back into the boat and cross to the other side of the lake, while he sent the people home. After sending them home, he went up into the hills by himself to pray. Night fell while he was there alone.

Meanwhile, the disciples were in trouble far away from land, for a strong wind had risen, and they were fighting heavy waves. About three o'clock in the morning Jesus came toward them, walking on the water. When the disciples saw him walking on the water, they were terrified. In their fear, they cried out, "It's a ghost!"

But Jesus spoke to them at once. "Don't be afraid," he said. "Take courage. I am here!"

Then Peter called to him, "Lord, if it's really you, tell me to come to you, walking on the water."

"Yes, come," Jesus said.

So Peter went over the side of the boat and walked on the water toward Jesus. But when he saw the strong wind and the waves, he was terrified and began to sink. "Save me, Lord!" he shouted.

Jesus immediately reached out and grabbed him. "You have

🔑 Key Verse

We are made right with God by placing our faith in Jesus Christ. And this is true for everyone who believes, no matter who we are.

Romans 3:22

so little faith," Jesus said. "Why did you doubt me?"

When they climbed back into the boat, the wind stopped. Then the disciples worshiped him. "You really are the Son of God!" they exclaimed.

It looks like Peter got carried away again.

Now What?

Peter was enthusiastic about leaping out of the boat to walk on the water to Jesus. And he was successful in staying on top of the water, too, until he started looking around at the waves and the wind. Then his faith faltered, becoming weaker and weaker until he sank into the water. What's the lesson from this? Keep your eyes and your thoughts directed toward Jesus. You can trust him, so stay focused on him instead of looking around at the problems that make you afraid.

76

A GOOD DEED DONE

What's Up

An expert in religious law asked Jesus how to have life that lasts forever. Jesus told him that the key is first to "love God with all your heart, soul, strength, and mind," and then to "love your neighbor as much as you love yourself." The man didn't quite seem to understand who his neighbor might be. So Jesus told him the story of the Good Samaritan to explain how to be a good neighbor.

Action Adventure from Luke 10:25-37

One day an expert in religious law stood up to test Jesus by asking him this question: "Teacher, what should I do to inherit eternal life?"

Jesus replied, "What does the law of Moses say? How do you read it?"

The man answered, "'You must love the LORD your God with all your heart, all your soul, all your strength, and all your mind.' And, 'Love your neighbor as yourself.'"

"Right!" Jesus told him. "Do this and you will live!"

The man wanted to justify his actions, so he asked Jesus, "And who is my neighbor?"

Jesus replied with a story: "A Jewish man was traveling on a trip from Jerusalem to Jericho, and he was attacked by bandits. They stripped him of his clothes, beat him up, and left him half dead beside the road.

"By chance a priest came along. But when he saw the man lying there, he crossed to the other side of the road and passed him by. A Temple assistant walked over and looked at him lying there, but he also passed by on the other side.

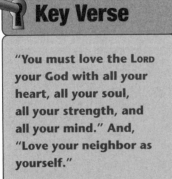

Key Verse

"You must love the LORD your God with all your heart, all your soul, all your strength, and all your mind." And, "Love your neighbor as yourself."

Luke 10:27

"Then a Samaritan came along. When he saw the man, he felt compassion for him. Going over to him, the Samaritan soothed his wounds with oil and wine and bandaged them. Then he put the man on his own donkey and took him to an inn, where he took care of him. The next day he handed the innkeeper two silver coins, telling him, 'Take care of this man. If his bill runs higher than this, I'll pay you the next time I'm here.'

"Now which of these three would you say was a neighbor to the man who was attacked by bandits?" Jesus asked.

It just looked like you needed some help!

The man replied, "The one who showed him mercy."

Then Jesus said, "Yes, now go and do the same."

Now What?

It's easy to be kind and helpful to a good friend. A good friend is usually someone who likes the same things you like and believes the same ways you believe. But the point of Jesus' story is that anyone you meet is your neighbor and deserves your kindness and care. The man in the story who had been hurt and the man from Samaria would have been considered enemies, but the Samaritan man showed the love of God by going out of his way to be kind and helpful. Look around you—does someone need a kind word or a bit of help? Perhaps you have ignored this person because he or she really isn't a friend. Maybe it's time to be a Good Samaritan!

77

A TALE OF TWO SISTERS

What's Up

Jesus and his disciples stopped to visit some good friends. Mary and Martha were sisters who were happy to welcome Jesus into their home. Martha fussed around the kitchen, preparing a big dinner for her guests. Mary didn't help her sister. She sat and listened to Jesus teach. Martha got upset and asked Jesus to tell Mary to get up and help. But Jesus didn't. His answer probably surprised Martha.

Action Adventure from Luke 10:38-42

As Jesus and the disciples continued on their way to Jerusalem, they came to a certain village where a woman named Martha welcomed him into her home.

Her sister, Mary, sat at the Lord's feet, listening to what he taught. But Martha was distracted by the big dinner she was preparing. She came to Jesus and said, "Lord, doesn't it seem unfair to you that my sister just sits here while I do all the work? Tell her to come and help me."

But the Lord said to her, "My dear Martha, you are worried and upset over all these details! There is only one thing worth being concerned about. Mary has discovered it, and it will not be taken away from her."

Key Verse

Be still, and know that I am God! I will be honored by every nation. I will be honored throughout the world.

Psalm 46:10

How about a little help in here?

Now What?

There is nothing wrong with being busy and helpful. Martha was a hard worker, and she wanted to make a nice dinner for Jesus. Would you have felt as upset with Mary as Martha did? It's not fun to be working hard when others are sitting around relaxing, is it? But what Martha didn't understand was the fact that it is very important to spend time with Jesus. It's important to listen to his teaching and just get to know him. You can do that by reading the Bible, praying, and just being quiet—no computer, no music, no TV. When you are quiet, you allow Jesus to speak to your heart. So there is a time to be busy and a time to be quiet.

78

LAZARUS LIVES!

What's Up

Jesus was good friends with Mary, Martha, and their brother, Lazarus. When Lazarus got very sick, his sisters sent for Jesus. They believed he could heal their brother. But Jesus didn't go to Lazarus right away. He wanted to glorify God by showing his power. So after Lazarus had been dead four days, Jesus arrived. Through his friend's death, Jesus was able to show God's life-giving power. Everyone who was at Lazarus's tomb was amazed!

Action Adventure from John 11:1-44

Lazarus was sick. His sisters, Mary and Martha, sent a message to Jesus telling him, "Lord, your friend is very sick."

But when Jesus heard about it he said, "Lazarus's sickness will not end in death. It happened so that the Son of God will receive glory." So he stayed where he was for the next two days. Finally, he said to his disciples, "Let's go to Judea. Our friend Lazarus has fallen asleep, but now I will go and wake him up."

They thought Jesus meant Lazarus was sleeping, but Jesus meant Lazarus had died.

So he told them, "Lazarus is dead. And for your sakes, I'm glad I wasn't there, for now you will really believe."

When Jesus arrived at Bethany, he was told that Lazarus had already been in his grave for four days. When Martha got word that Jesus was coming, she went to meet him. Martha said to Jesus, "Lord, if only you had been here, my brother would not have died. But even now I know that God will give you whatever you ask."

Jesus told her, "Your brother will rise again. I am the resurrection and the life. Anyone who believes in me will live, even after dying. Do you believe this, Martha?"

"Yes," she told him. "I have always believed you are the

🔑 Key Verse

Death is swallowed up in victory. O death, where is your victory? O death, where is your sting?

1 Corinthians 15:54-55

Messiah, the Son of God." Then she called Mary aside and told her, "The Teacher wants to see you." So Mary immediately went to him.

When Mary saw Jesus, she fell at his feet and said, "Lord, if only you had been here, my brother would not have died."

When Jesus saw her weeping and saw the people with her, he was deeply troubled. "Where have you put him?" he asked.

They told him, "Lord, come and see." Then Jesus wept.

Jesus arrived at the tomb, a cave with a stone rolled across its entrance. "Roll the stone aside," Jesus told them.

But Martha protested, "Lord, he has been dead for four days. The smell will be terrible."

Jesus responded, "Didn't I tell you that you would see God's glory if you believe?" So they rolled the stone aside. Then Jesus said, "Father, thank

I believed Jesus could have saved him, but this is over the top!

you for hearing me. You always hear me, but I said it out loud for the sake of all these people standing here, so that they will believe you sent me."

Then Jesus shouted, "Lazarus, come out!" And the dead man came out, his hands and feet bound in graveclothes, his face wrapped in a headcloth. Jesus told them, "Unwrap him and let him go!"

Now What?

What a cool story, right? Jesus was sad, but he knew that he has power over death. He knew that Mary, Martha, and all their friends who were there to comfort them would see that power and believe in it when Lazarus walked out of the tomb! Jesus still has power over death. Once you accept him as your Savior, you can know you will live forever with him in heaven after your time on this earth ends. What a wonderful promise!

79

A LOST SON RETURNS

What's Up

Jesus often taught lessons by telling stories. One story that explained God's forgiveness and love was about a father who welcomed home a son who had been gone for a long time. This son is often called the Prodigal Son. When the son came home and asked his dad to forgive him, his father not only forgave him but had a party to celebrate his return!

Action Adventure from Luke 15:11-32

Jesus told this story: "A man had two sons. The younger son told his father, 'I want my share of your estate now.' So his father agreed to divide his wealth between his sons.

"A few days later this younger son moved to a distant land and wasted his money in wild living. About the time his money ran out, a great famine swept over the land, and he began to starve. He persuaded a local farmer to hire him, and the man sent him to feed the pigs. The young man became so hungry that even the pods he was feeding the pigs looked good. But no one gave him anything.

"He said to himself, 'At home even the hired servants have food, and here I am dying of hunger! I will go home and say, "Father, I have sinned against both heaven and you, and am no longer worthy of being called your son. Please take me on as a hired servant."'

"So he returned home. While he was still a long way off, his father saw him coming. Filled with love and compassion, he ran to his son, embraced him, and kissed him. His son said to him, 'Father, I have sinned against both heaven and you, and I am no longer worthy of being called your son.'

"But his father said to the

Key Verse

We must celebrate with a feast, for this son of mine was dead and has now returned to life. He was lost, but now he is found.

Luke 15:23-24

servants, 'Bring the finest robe and put it on him. Get a ring for his finger and sandals for his feet. Kill the calf we have been fattening. We must celebrate with a feast, for this son of mine was dead and has now returned to life. He was lost, but now he is found.' So the party began.

"Meanwhile, the older son was in the fields working. When he returned home, he heard music. He asked one of the servants what was going on. 'Your brother is back,' he was told. 'We are celebrating because of his safe return.'

"The older brother was angry and wouldn't go in. His father begged him, but he replied, 'All these years I've slaved for you and never refused to do a thing you told me to. And you never gave me even one goat for a feast with my friends. Yet when

I guess I wasn't as smart as I thought I was!

this son of yours comes back, you celebrate!'

"His father said to him, 'Look, dear son, you have always stayed by me, and everything I have is yours. We had to celebrate this happy day. For your brother was dead and has come back to life! He was lost, but now he is found!'"

Now What?

This story helps us understand that God is always ready to love us and forgive us. When someone turns away from sin and gives his or her heart to God, this person is immediately forgiven. And God celebrates this new member of his family! He is excited when even only one person comes to him. And, if you've already accepted Jesus but have turned away from him to do your own thing, never fear! Come back to God, ask him to forgive you, and know that he will. He will forgive you, love you, and gladly welcome you back!

80

A SAVIOR'S GLORY

What's Up

Peter, James, and John were three of Jesus' disciples, but they were also three of his best friends. One day Jesus took these three men with him up to the top of a mountain. As the three friends watched, Jesus' appearance was transformed—it changed. Then Moses and Elijah came to talk with him. Peter, James, and John were amazed. When they went back down the mountain, Jesus told them not to tell anyone what had happened.

Action Adventure from Matthew 17:1-13

Jesus took Peter and the two brothers, James and John, and led them up a high mountain to be alone. As the men watched, Jesus' appearance was transformed so that his face shone like the sun, and his clothes became as white as light. Suddenly, Moses and Elijah appeared and began talking with Jesus.

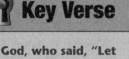

Key Verse

God, who said, "Let there be light in the darkness," has made this light shine in our hearts so we could know the glory of God that is seen in the face of Jesus Christ.

2 Corinthians 4:6

Peter exclaimed, "Lord, it's wonderful for us to be here! If you want, I'll make three shelters as memorials—one for you, one for Moses, and one for Elijah."

But even as he spoke, a bright cloud overshadowed them, and a voice from the cloud said, "This is my dearly loved Son, who brings me great joy. Listen to him." The disciples were terrified and fell face down on the ground.

Then Jesus came over and touched them. "Get up," he said. "Don't be afraid." And when they looked up, Moses and Elijah were gone, and they saw only Jesus.

As they went back down the mountain, Jesus commanded them, "Don't tell anyone what you have seen until the Son of Man has been raised from the dead."

Then his disciples asked him, "Why do the teachers of religious law insist that Elijah must return before the Messiah comes?"

Jesus replied, "Elijah is indeed coming first to get everything ready. But I tell you, Elijah has already come, but he wasn't recognized, and they chose to abuse him. And in the same way they will also make the Son of Man suffer." Then the disciples realized he was talking about John the Baptist.

He doesn't have to worry about my telling anyone. Nobody would believe it, anyway.

Now What?

When Jesus took his special friends up on the mountain with him, he knew that something amazing was going to happen there. He wanted his friends to see his glory. He wanted them to know how much God loved him. God the Father does love Jesus, his Son, and is very pleased with all of his work. When you think about how much God loves Jesus, does that make you want to respect and honor him more? It should. It's important to understand the relationship between God and his Son, Jesus.

81

FROM NIGHT TO SIGHT

What's Up

Jesus and his disciples arrived in Jericho with crowds surrounding him as usual. As he walked through the town, a man who was blind began shouting to him, asking him for mercy. The people around the blind man told him to be quiet, but he just shouted louder. Jesus heard him and called him to come over to him. He asked what the man wanted him to do. The blind man was excited to discover that Jesus cared!

Action Adventure from Mark 10:46-52

They reached Jericho, and as Jesus and his disciples left town, a large crowd followed him. A blind beggar named Bartimaeus was sitting beside the road. When Bartimaeus heard that Jesus of Nazareth was nearby, he began to shout, "Jesus, Son of David, have mercy on me!"

"Be quiet!" many of the people yelled at him.

But he only shouted louder, "Son of David, have mercy on me!"

When Jesus heard him, he stopped and said, "Tell him to come here."

So they called the blind man. "Cheer up," they said. "Come on, he's calling you!" Bartimaeus threw aside his coat, jumped up, and came to Jesus.

"What do you want me to do for you?" Jesus asked.

"My rabbi," the blind man said, "I want to see!"

And Jesus said to him, "Go, for your faith has healed you." Instantly the man could see, and he followed Jesus down the road.

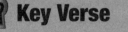

Key Verse

Let your roots grow down into him, and let your lives be built on him. Then your faith will grow strong in the truth you were taught, and you will overflow with thankfulness.

Colossians 2:7

I guess he cares about everyone!

Now What?

Faith can change everything. Bartimaeus believed Jesus could heal him. He believed it so strongly that he kept crying out to Jesus even when people around him told him to be quiet. He probably thought this was his one chance to get his sight back. How strong is your faith? When you pray to Jesus for help, do you really believe he can do what you ask? If your friends tell you to stop praying or to leave God alone, do you listen to them? Or do you continue going to God because you believe—you have faith—that he can help you?

82

ZACCHAEUS

What's Up

When Jesus traveled through Jericho and met a blind man who wanted to see, Jesus also met a tax collector. This man was named Zacchaeus. He was a short man and couldn't see over the crowd. So Zacchaeus climbed up in a tree to be able to see Jesus. He didn't expect Jesus to look up in the tree and find him. But he did. And Jesus told Zacchaeus he was going home with him. Why would Jesus want to do that?

Action Adventure from Luke 19:1-10

Jesus entered Jericho and made his way through the town. There was a man there named Zacchaeus. He was the chief tax collector in the region, and he had become very rich. He tried to get a look at Jesus, but he was too short to see over the crowd. So he ran ahead and climbed a sycamore-fig tree beside the road, for Jesus was going to pass that way.

When Jesus came by, he looked up at Zacchaeus and called him by name. "Zacchaeus!" he said. "Quick, come down! I must be a guest in your home today."

Zacchaeus quickly climbed down and took Jesus to his house in great excitement and joy. But the people were displeased. "He has gone to be the guest of a sinner," they grumbled.

Meanwhile, Zacchaeus stood before the Lord and said, "I will give half my wealth to the poor, Lord, and if I have cheated people on their taxes, I will give them back four times as much!"

Jesus responded, "Salvation has come to this home today, for this man has shown himself to be a true son of Abraham. For the Son of Man came to seek and save those who are lost."

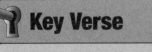
Key Verse

The Son of Man came to seek and save those who are lost.

Luke 19:10

How can he stand to be with a sinner like him?

Now What?

Tax collectors in Bible times were very unpopular because they often cheated people. No one would have wanted to help Zacchaeus get through the crowd to see Jesus. But after Jesus talked with the tax collector, he was a changed man who wanted to serve and obey Jesus. How did you change when you met Jesus? Did you want to treat others with respect and fairness? Did you want to be more honest? Did you want to serve him and obey him? Meeting Jesus should lead to changes in each of our lives—changes that other people notice.

83

HEADING TO JERUSALEM

What's Up

The end of Jesus' life on earth was coming soon. He knew it, but his disciples and other followers didn't quite get it. As Jesus entered Jerusalem riding on a borrowed donkey, crowds of people cheered and laid their coats on the road for him to ride over. They shouted praise to the Son of God. Others in the town wondered what was going on.

Action Adventure from Matthew 21:1-11

As Jesus and the disciples approached Jerusalem, they came to the Mount of Olives. Jesus sent two of them on ahead. "Go into the village over there," he said. "As soon as you enter it, you will see a donkey tied there, with its colt beside it. Untie them and bring them to me. If anyone asks what you are doing, just say, 'The Lord needs them,' and he will immediately let you take them."

This took place to fulfill the prophecy that said, "Tell the people of Jerusalem, 'Look, your King is coming to you. He is humble, riding on a donkey—riding on a donkey's colt.'"

The two disciples did as Jesus commanded. They brought the donkey and the colt to him and threw their garments over the colt, and he sat on it.

Most of the crowd spread their garments on the road ahead of him, and others cut branches from the trees and spread them on the road. Jesus was in the center of the procession, and the people all around him were shouting, "Praise God for the Son of David! Blessings on the one who comes in the name of the LORD! Praise God in highest heaven!"

The entire city of Jerusalem was in an uproar as he entered. "Who is this?" they asked.

Key Verse

Praise God for the Son of David! Blessings on the one who comes in the name of the LORD! Praise God in highest heaven!

Matthew 21:9

And the crowds replied, "It's Jesus, the prophet from Nazareth in Galilee."

I'm not sure this is going to look very kingly.

Now What?

Jesus rode into Jerusalem, not as a king, but as a humble servant riding on a donkey. He didn't come to earth to be a king, as the crowds of people were trying to make him be. He came to earth to save lost people and to serve those who need him. However, as he rode the donkey into town, the people cheered for him. They thought he was going to be their king. He is . . . but not the kind of king they expected. Is Jesus your heavenly king? Does he rule your life? Do you shout his praises aloud? Do your friends know that you honor and serve the King of heaven?

84

THE LAST SUPPER

What's Up

Jesus and his disciples sat down together to eat the Passover meal. It was a special meal to help them remember when their relatives from long ago—their ancestors—were slaves in Egypt. After eating the Passover meal, Moses had led God's people out of Egypt. Now, during the supper Jesus told his disciples that he knew one of them would betray him—turn his back on him. They were all upset by this and wanted to know which of them would do such a thing. It was Judas. The supper was the last one that the disciples would share with Jesus before he died, but they didn't know this yet.

Action Adventure from Matthew 26:17-30

The disciples came to Jesus and asked, "Where do you want us to prepare the Passover meal for you?"

"As you go into the city," he told them, "you will see a certain man. Tell him, 'The Teacher says: My time has come, and I will eat the Passover meal with my disciples at your house.'" So the disciples did as Jesus told them and prepared the Passover meal there.

When it was evening, Jesus sat down at the table with the twelve disciples. While they were eating, he said, "I tell you the truth, one of you will betray me."

Greatly distressed, each one asked in turn, "Am I the one, Lord?"

He replied, "One of you who has just eaten from this bowl with me will betray me. For the Son of Man must die, as the

Key Verse

He took a cup of wine and gave thanks to God for it. He gave it to them and said, "Each of you drink from it, for this is my blood, which confirms the covenant between God and his people. It is poured out as a sacrifice to forgive the sins of many."

Matthew 26:27-28

Scriptures declared long ago. But how terrible it will be for the one who betrays him."

Judas, the one who would betray him, also asked, "Rabbi, am I the one?"

And Jesus told him, "You have said it."

As they were eating, Jesus took some bread and blessed it. Then he broke it in pieces and gave it to the disciples, saying, "Take this and eat it, for this is my body."

And he took a cup of wine and gave thanks to God for it. He gave it to them and said, "Each of you drink from it, for this is my blood, which confirms the covenant between God and his people. It is poured out as

I think something is up!

a sacrifice to forgive the sins of many. Mark my words—I will not drink wine again until the day I drink it new with you in my Father's Kingdom."

Then they sang a hymn and went out to the Mount of Olives.

Now What?

The disciples did not understand that Jesus was going to have to die. His words about the bread being his body and the wine being his blood must have been hard for them to understand. Now those words are repeated nearly every time we take Communion, and we know they refer to Jesus' death on the cross. When you hear Jesus' words, do you thank him for the sacrifice of his life that makes your salvation possible? Don't take your salvation lightly. Don't take Communion lightly. These things are available to you because of the suffering and death of Jesus . . . in your place.

85

ARREST IN GETHSEMANE

What's Up

Jesus took his disciples to the Garden of Gethsemane after they ate their last meal together. He wanted to spend some time in prayer, and he wanted his disciples to pray also. However, they kept falling asleep. Each time Jesus returned from his prayer time, he woke them up. After the third time he woke them, Judas led a group of soldiers right over to Jesus. Judas kissed him on the cheek. That's how Judas betrayed Jesus—acting as if he loved him but really showing the soldiers which one was Jesus. Then the soldiers arrested him.

Action Adventure from Mark 14:32-50

They went to the olive grove called Gethsemane, and Jesus said, "Sit here while I go and pray." He took Peter, James, and John with him, and he became deeply troubled. He told them, "My soul is crushed with grief to the point of death. Stay here and keep watch with me."

He went on a little farther and fell to the ground. He prayed that, if it were possible, the awful hour awaiting him might pass him by. "Abba, Father," he cried out, "everything is possible for you. Please take this cup of suffering away from me. Yet I want your will to be done, not mine."

Then he returned and found the disciples asleep. He said to Peter, "Couldn't you watch with me even one hour? Keep watch and pray, so that you will not give in to temptation. For the spirit is willing, but the body is weak."

Jesus left them again and prayed the same prayer. When he returned to them again, he found them sleeping, for they couldn't keep their eyes open.

Key Verse

"Abba, Father," he cried out, "everything is possible for you. Please take this cup of suffering away from me. Yet I want your will to be done, not mine."

Mark 14:36

When he returned to them the third time, he said, "Go ahead and sleep. Have your rest. But no—the time has come. The Son of Man is betrayed into the hands of sinners. Look, my betrayer is here!"

Even as Jesus said this, Judas, one of the twelve disciples, arrived with a crowd of men armed with swords and clubs. They had been sent by the leading priests, the teachers of religious law, and the elders. The traitor, Judas, had given them a signal: "You will know which one to arrest when I greet him with a kiss." As soon as they arrived, Judas walked up to Jesus. "Rabbi!" he exclaimed, and gave him the kiss.

Then the others grabbed Jesus and arrested him. But one of the men with Jesus pulled out his sword and struck the high priest's

Okay, now I see what he meant!

slave, slashing off his ear. Jesus asked them, "Am I dangerous, that you come with swords and clubs to arrest me? Why didn't you arrest me in the Temple? I was there among you teaching every day. But these things are happening to fulfill what the Scriptures say about me."

Then all his disciples ran away.

Now What?

Jesus always knew that he was going to suffer and die for everyone's sins. So, when he went to the Garden of Gethsemane, he knew that what was ahead for him was going to be terrible. He even asked if he could skip it. But the important part of his prayer is this: "I want your will to be done, not mine." Jesus obeyed his Father in heaven, for he knew that dying on the cross was the main reason that he had been sent to earth. Sometimes life is hard, and even the things God wants you to do could be kind of difficult. Do you always obey God—even when it's hard?

86

DENYING A FRIEND

What's Up

Jesus warned his followers that they would desert him when times got hard. He knew that Peter would even say he didn't know Jesus. Peter couldn't begin to imagine that would actually happen. But after Jesus was arrested—and while he was being questioned by the authorities— Peter did deny even knowing Jesus . . . three times!

Action Adventure from Matthew 26:31-35, 57-58, 69-75

On the way [to Gethsemane], Jesus told [his disciples], "Tonight all of you will desert me. For the Scriptures say, 'God will strike the Shepherd, and the sheep of the flock will be scattered.' But after I have been raised from the dead, I will go ahead of you to Galilee and meet you there."

Peter declared, "Even if everyone else deserts you, I will never desert you."

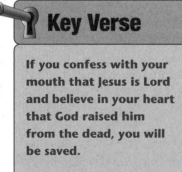

Key Verse

If you confess with your mouth that Jesus is Lord and believe in your heart that God raised him from the dead, you will be saved.

Romans 10:9

Jesus replied, "I tell you the truth, Peter—this very night, before the rooster crows, you will deny three times that you even know me."

"No!" Peter insisted. "Even if I have to die with you, I will never deny you!" And all the other disciples vowed the same.

Then the people who had arrested Jesus led him to the home of Caiaphas, the high priest, where the teachers of religious law and the elders had gathered. Meanwhile, Peter followed him at a distance and came to the high priest's courtyard. He went in and sat with the guards and waited to see how it would all end. A servant girl came over and said to him, "You were one of those with Jesus the Galilean."

But Peter denied it in front

of everyone. "I don't know what you're talking about," he said.

Later, out by the gate, another servant girl noticed him and said to those standing around, "This man was with Jesus of Nazareth."

Again Peter denied it, this time with an oath. "I don't even know the man," he said.

A little later some of the other bystanders came over to Peter and said, "You must be one of them; we can tell by your Galilean accent."

Peter swore, "A curse on me if I'm lying—I don't know the man!" And immediately the rooster crowed.

Suddenly, Jesus' words

I can't believe I let him down that easily!

flashed through Peter's mind: "Before the rooster crows, you will deny three times that you even know me." And he went away, weeping bitterly.

Now What?

Peter was so certain that he would never deny Jesus. But when the going got tough, he did deny knowing anything about his friend . . . three different times. If you ever have felt you were in danger because of your beliefs, you know it can be tempting to let the beliefs go. Or you may think, *Well, I can say what people want me to say but still believe in my heart.* Yeah, sure—not true. It doesn't really work that way. When you believe in Jesus and want to live for him, it will show on the outside as well as the inside. Taking a stand for him can be hard when your faith is questioned. But if you don't speak up, you are denying Jesus just as Peter did.

JESUS ON TRIAL

What's Up

Jesus was an innocent man, not guilty of doing anything wrong. But the religious leaders were jealous of him and didn't want people to believe in him. So they had him arrested. Jesus was put through a hurried trial in the middle of the night. Even though Pilate, the Roman governor, could find no reason for Jesus to be crucified—to be put to death on a cross— the people cried out, "Crucify him!" Every year Pilate set one prisoner free during Passover. The crowd chose Barabbas, who had killed a man, to be freed instead of Jesus.

Action Adventure from Matthew 27:1-26

Very early in the morning the priests met again to lay plans for putting Jesus to death. They bound him and took him to Pilate, the Roman governor. When Judas, who had betrayed him, realized that Jesus had been condemned to die, he took the thirty pieces of silver back to the priests and the elders. "I have sinned," he declared, "for I have betrayed an innocent man."

"What do we care?" they retorted. "That's your problem."

🔑 Key Verse

What should I do with Jesus who is called the Messiah?

Matthew 27:22

Judas threw the silver coins down in the Temple and went out and hanged himself.

The priests picked up the coins. "It wouldn't be right to put this money in the Temple treasury," they said, "since it was payment for murder." They decided to buy the potter's field, and they made it into a cemetery for foreigners.

Now Jesus was standing before Pilate, the Roman governor. "Are you the king of the Jews?" the governor asked him.

Jesus replied, "You have said it."

But when the priests made their accusations against him, Jesus remained silent. "Don't you hear all these charges they are bringing against you?" Pilate demanded. But Jesus made no response.

It was the governor's custom each year during the Passover celebration to release one prisoner to the crowd—anyone they wanted. This year there was a prisoner named Barabbas. As the crowds gathered before Pilate's house that morning, he asked them, "Which one do you want me to release to you—Barabbas, or Jesus who is called the Messiah?"

The priests persuaded the crowd to ask for Barabbas to be released.

Pilate responded, "Then what should I do with Jesus who is called the Messiah?"

They shouted back, "Crucify him!"

I can't figure out what he has done wrong!

Pilate sent for a bowl of water and washed his hands before the crowd, saying, "I am innocent of this man's blood."

So Pilate released Barabbas to them. He ordered Jesus flogged with a lead-tipped whip, then turned him over to the Roman soldiers to be crucified.

Now What?

Pilate knew that Jesus was innocent of any crime. He saw no reason for Jesus to be arrested. The religious leaders, who wanted Jesus out of the way, got the crowd so upset and so angry that they called for Jesus' crucifixion. It's possible that some of the people didn't really want Jesus to die. But they got caught up with the crowd, which became a wild mob, totally out of control. That's a warning for you. Don't get caught up in the actions of a wild crowd so that you try to get something you don't even want. Jesus could have called angels to save him from the crowd. But he didn't. He knew that God, his Father, had a plan, and he was doing his part to make it happen.

88

DEATH OF A SAVIOR

What's Up

After Pilate washed his hands of Jesus' trial, things seemed to happen at warp speed. The soldiers did whatever they wanted to make fun of Jesus. Then they nailed him to a cross. Jesus, who was not only an innocent man but also the pure and blameless Son of God, died for the sins of all people everywhere.

Action Adventure from Matthew 27:27-66

Soldiers put a scarlet robe on [Jesus]. They wove thorn branches into a crown and put it on his head. Then they taunted, "Hail! King of the Jews!" When they were tired of mocking him, they put his own clothes on him again. Then they led him away to be crucified.

They came across a man named Simon and forced him to carry Jesus' cross to Golgotha (which means "Place of the Skull").

Key Verse

God loved the world so much that he gave his one and only Son, so that everyone who believes in him will not perish but have eternal life.

John 3:16

After they nailed him to the cross, the soldiers gambled for his clothes by throwing dice. A sign was fastened above Jesus' head. It read: "This is Jesus, the King of the Jews." Two revolutionaries were crucified with him, one on his right and one on his left.

The people shouted, "You said you were going to destroy the Temple and rebuild it in three days. If you are the Son of God, save yourself and come down from the cross!"

The priests also mocked Jesus. "He saved others, but he can't save himself!"

At noon, darkness fell across the whole land. At about three o'clock, Jesus called out with a loud voice, "My God, my God, why have you abandoned me?"

Then Jesus released his spirit. At that moment the curtain in the Temple was torn in two, from top to bottom. The earth shook, rocks split apart, and tombs opened. The bodies of many godly men and women who had died were raised from the dead.

The Roman soldiers at the crucifixion were terrified by all that had happened. They said, "This man truly was the Son of God!"

Joseph from Arimathea went to Pilate and asked for Jesus' body. Joseph wrapped it in clean linen cloth. He placed it in his own new tomb. Then he rolled a great stone across the entrance and left. Both Mary Magdalene and the other Mary were sitting across from the tomb and watching.

The priests and Pharisees went to see Pilate. "Sir, we request that you seal the

This should be the end of the problem!

tomb until the third day. This will prevent his disciples from coming and stealing his body and then telling everyone he was raised from the dead."

Pilate replied, "Take guards and secure it the best you can." So they sealed the tomb and posted guards to protect it.

Now What?

When Jesus came to earth as a baby, many people understood that he was the Messiah—the one God had promised to send to save his people. Now, the reality of what that meant was happening. Jesus could have called angels to save him. God could have rescued him from his enemies with a miracle. But none of that happened because the plan all along was for Jesus to die for everyone's sins. Then we could be friends with God and live in heaven with him forever. This story of Jesus' death on the cross shows God's amazing love for all people . . . and his love for you.

89

JESUS IS ALIVE!

What's Up

The tomb where Jesus' body was buried was a cave. On Sunday, after the Sabbath was over, some women who had been friends of Jesus planned to put oils and perfumes on his body. This was their usual practice. Mary Magdalene got to the tomb before anyone else and had a great surprise— Jesus' body was gone! Even though Jesus had told his followers that he would come back to life, none of them really expected him to do it. But then Jesus appeared to Mary and told her that he really was alive. So she ran to tell his other friends!

Action Adventure from John 20:1-18

Early on Sunday morning, while it was still dark, Mary Magdalene came to the tomb and found that the stone had been rolled away from the entrance. She ran and found Simon Peter and the other disciple, the one whom Jesus loved. She said, "They have taken the Lord's body out of the tomb, and we don't know where they have put him!"

Key Verse

Jesus told her, "I am the resurrection and the life. Anyone who believes in me will live, even after dying."

John 11:25

Peter and the other disciple started for the tomb. The other disciple reached the tomb first. He looked in and saw the linen wrappings lying there, but he didn't go in. Then Peter went inside. He noticed the cloth that had covered Jesus' head was folded up and lying apart from the other wrappings. Then the disciple who had reached the tomb first also went in, and he saw and believed—for until then they still hadn't understood the Scriptures that said Jesus must rise from the dead. Then they went home.

Mary was outside the tomb crying, and she looked in. She saw two white-robed angels, one sitting at the head and the other at the foot of the place where the body of Jesus had been lying. "Dear woman, why are you crying?" the angels asked her.

"Because they have taken away my Lord," she replied, "and I don't know where they have put him."

She turned to leave and saw someone standing there. It was Jesus, but she didn't recognize him. "Why are you crying?" Jesus asked her. "Who are you looking for?"

She thought he was the gardener. "Sir," she said, "if you have taken him away, tell me where you have put him, and I will go and get him."

"Mary!" Jesus said.

She turned to him and cried out, "Rabboni!" (which is Hebrew for "Teacher").

"Don't cling to me," Jesus

I think this is all part of the plan!

said, "for I haven't yet ascended to the Father. But go find my brothers and tell them, 'I am ascending to my Father and your Father, to my God and your God.'"

Mary Magdalene found the disciples and told them, "I have seen the Lord!" Then she gave them his message.

Now What?

Jesus' friends went from thinking they were living through the saddest day they could imagine to realizing it was the happiest, most unusual, amazing day they could have dreamed of. They probably were still thinking through Jesus' death and how to deal with that when all of a sudden they found out that he was alive! Jesus' victory over death is a promise to his followers that they will have victory over death too! He promises that each one who follows him will live forever in heaven with him. How cool is that!

90

ON THE ROAD TO EMMAUS

What's Up

Two of Jesus' followers were walking to the village of Emmaus. It was the afternoon of the day when Jesus came back to life. Suddenly, a third person was walking with them. It was Jesus! They didn't recognize him, though, so they told him about all the things that had happened. He asked questions and then went home with them. When they sat down to eat, Jesus prayed. Then they knew that it was Jesus with them.

Action Adventure from Luke 24:13-35

Two of Jesus' followers were walking to the village of Emmaus, seven miles from Jerusalem. As they walked along they were talking about everything that had happened. Jesus himself suddenly came and began walking with them. But God kept them from recognizing him.

He asked them, "What are you discussing as you walk along?"

One of them replied, "You must be the only person in Jerusalem who hasn't heard about all the things that have happened there the last few days."

"What things?" Jesus asked.

"The things that happened to Jesus from Nazareth," they said. "He was a prophet who did powerful miracles, and he was a mighty teacher. But our religious leaders crucified him. We had hoped he was the Messiah who had come to rescue Israel. This all happened three days ago. Then some women from our group were at his tomb early this morning, and they came back with an amazing report. They said his body was missing, and they had seen angels who told them Jesus is alive! Some of our men ran out to see, and sure enough, his body was gone, just as the women had said."

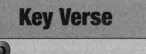

Key Verse

The gatekeeper opens the gate for him, and the sheep recognize his voice and come to him. He calls his own sheep by name and leads them out.

John 10:3

By this time they were nearing Emmaus and the end of their journey. Jesus acted as if he were going on, but they begged him, "Stay the night with us, since it is getting late." So he went home with them. As they sat down to eat, he took the bread and blessed it. Then he broke it and gave it to them. Suddenly, their eyes were opened, and they recognized him. And at that moment he disappeared!

They aren't going to believe this!

They said to each other, "Didn't our hearts burn within us as he talked with us on the road and explained the Scriptures to us?" And within the hour they were on their way back to Jerusalem. There they found the eleven disciples and the others who had gathered with them, who said, "The Lord has really risen! He appeared to Peter." Then the two from Emmaus told their story of how Jesus had appeared to them as they were walking along the road, and how they had recognized him as he was breaking the bread.

Now What?

Does it seem hard to believe that these two followers of Jesus didn't recognize him? Don't blame them too much. Do you think you would recognize Jesus if he came and walked along with you today? The Bible tells us that Jesus' followers will recognize his voice, just as a sheep knows its own shepherd's voice. But, for that to happen, you must be spending time getting to know Jesus. Just as you recognize a friend's voice because you've spent time together, you will know Jesus' voice because you have spent time reading the Bible. You may not hear a real voice, but you will "hear" thoughts in your mind. And you will know which ones come from Jesus.

91

THOMAS DOUBTS

What's Up

Jesus' disciples stayed together and met in a locked room because they were afraid that the Jewish leaders might want to put them to death too. It was evening now of the day when Jesus came back to life. Suddenly, Jesus was standing there with them! He really was alive! But one of the disciples, Thomas, wasn't with the others that night. He couldn't believe Jesus was alive unless he saw it for himself. So . . . Jesus appeared to his disciples again!

Action Adventure from John 20:19-29

That Sunday evening the disciples were meeting behind locked doors because they were afraid of the Jewish leaders. Suddenly, Jesus was standing there among them! "Peace be with you," he said. As he spoke, he showed them the wounds in his hands and his side. They were filled with joy when they saw the Lord! Again he said, "Peace be with you. As the Father has sent me, so I am sending you."

One of the twelve disciples, Thomas (nicknamed the Twin), was not with the others when Jesus came. They told him, "We have seen the Lord!"

But he replied, "I won't believe it unless I see the nail wounds in his hands, put my fingers into them, and place my hand into the wound in his side."

Eight days later the disciples were together again, and this time Thomas was with them. The doors were locked; but suddenly, as before, Jesus was standing among them. "Peace be with you," he said. Then he said to Thomas, "Put your finger here, and look at my hands. Put your hand into the wound in my side. Don't be faithless any longer. Believe!"

Key Verse

Jesus told him, "You believe because you have seen me. Blessed are those who believe without seeing me."

John 20:29

"My Lord and my God!" Thomas exclaimed.

Then Jesus told him, "You believe because you have seen me. Blessed are those who believe without seeing me."

Wow! That's powerful proof.

Now What?

Some people, like Thomas, need proof that something is true before they can believe it. They do not have a lot of faith. Jesus is glad when we believe in him—we believe that he is God's Son, that he died for our sins, and that he rose again to life. We believe this even though we haven't actually seen him in person or touched him or perhaps even heard his voice. We believe because we have faith. We are blessed with joy and peace because of that faith. Do you believe? Tell Jesus so!

92

BREAKFAST WITH THE SAVIOR

What's Up

Several of Jesus' disciples had been fishermen before they began following him. One day after Jesus came back to life, some of them were fishing on the Sea of Galilee. But they didn't catch anything. When they came to shore, Jesus was there. He told them to fish again, and they caught many fish. Then Jesus gave Peter a pop quiz to see how much he loved him!

Action Adventure from John 21:1-19

Jesus appeared to the disciples beside the Sea of Galilee. Peter said, "I'm going fishing."

"We'll come, too," they all said. So they went out in the boat, but they caught nothing all night.

At dawn Jesus was standing on the beach, but the disciples couldn't see who he was. He called out, "Have you caught any fish?"

"No," they replied.

Then he said, "Throw out your net on the right-hand side of the boat, and you'll get some!" So they did, and they couldn't haul in the net because there were so many fish in it.

When Peter heard that it was the Lord, he jumped into the water and headed to shore. The others stayed with the boat and pulled the loaded net to the shore, for they were only about a hundred yards from shore. When they got there, they found breakfast waiting for them—fish cooking over a charcoal fire, and some bread.

"Bring some of the fish you've

🔑 Key Verse

A third time he asked him, "Simon son of John, do you love me?" Peter was hurt that Jesus asked the question a third time. He said, "Lord, you know everything. You know that I love you." Jesus said, "Then feed my sheep."

John 21:17

just caught," Jesus said. So Simon Peter went aboard and dragged the net to the shore. There were 153 large fish, and yet the net hadn't torn.

"Now come and have some breakfast!" Jesus said. None of the disciples dared to ask him, "Who are you?" They knew it was the Lord. Then Jesus served them the bread and the fish. This was the third time Jesus had appeared to his disciples since he had been raised from the dead.

After breakfast Jesus asked Peter, "Simon son of John, do you love me more than these?"

"Yes, Lord," Peter replied, "you know I love you."

"Then feed my lambs," Jesus told him.

Jesus repeated the question: "Simon son of John, do you love me?"

"Yes, Lord," Peter said, "you know I love you."

This seems like overkill!

"Then take care of my sheep," Jesus said.

A third time he asked him, "Simon son of John, do you love me?"

Peter was hurt that Jesus asked the question a third time. He said, "Lord, you know everything. You know that I love you."

Jesus said, "Then feed my sheep. Follow me."

Now What?

It's not enough just to say that you love Jesus. Words are not enough. Even feelings are not enough. Loving Jesus demands some action.
Jesus asked Peter if he really loved him. When Peter said yes, Jesus told him to do something—"feed my sheep." He wasn't talking about animals. He was talking about people who need to learn more about God and need to be fed the truth of God's love. Loving Jesus means working for Jesus, telling others about him. How can you serve him?

93

JESUS GOES HOME

What's Up

After Jesus rose from the dead, he appeared to his disciples—also called his apostles—over the next 40 days. The last time he saw his followers, he told them to stay in Jerusalem until God sent them the Holy Spirit as he had promised. He told them that the Holy Spirit would give them the power they needed to be his witnesses, telling others about him around the whole earth. Then, right before their eyes, he was taken to heaven!

Action Adventure from Acts 1:1-11

Jesus was taken up to heaven after giving his chosen apostles further instructions through the Holy Spirit. During the forty days after his crucifixion, he appeared to the apostles from time to time, and he proved to them in many ways that he was actually alive. And he talked to them about the Kingdom of God.

Key Verse

You will receive power when the Holy Spirit comes upon you.
And you will be my witnesses, telling people about me everywhere—
in Jerusalem, throughout Judea, in Samaria, and to the ends of the earth.

Acts 1:8

Once when he was eating with them, he commanded them, "Do not leave Jerusalem until the Father sends you the gift he promised, as I told you before. John baptized with water, but in just a few days you will be baptized with the Holy Spirit."

So when the apostles were with Jesus, they kept asking him, "Lord, has the time come for you to free Israel and restore our kingdom?"

He replied, "The Father alone has the authority to set those dates and times, and they are not for you to know. But you will receive power when the Holy Spirit comes upon you. And you will be my witnesses, telling people about me everywhere— in Jerusalem, throughout Judea, in Samaria, and to the ends of the earth."

After saying this, he was taken up into a cloud while they were watching, and they could no longer see him. As they strained to see him rising into heaven, two white-robed men suddenly stood among them. "Men of Galilee," they said, "why are you standing here staring into heaven? Jesus has been taken from you into heaven, but someday he will return from heaven in the same way you saw him go!"

Okay, I guess it is time for us to get to work!

Now What?

Jesus' work on earth was done. So he went back to heaven. But after he left, God sent the Holy Spirit to be with his followers, because there was still work to be done. The Holy Spirit would give Jesus' friends power to work for him. The Holy Spirit also gives you power, because he wants you to be his witness too. You can tell people around you about Jesus' love and maybe someday even travel to other cities or countries to help do his work! Call on the power of the Holy Spirit. He is there for you!

HERE COMES THE HOLY SPIRIT!

What's Up

Jesus had promised that the Holy Spirit was coming to his followers. The day when the Holy Spirit came, all the believers were together. There was a loud noise, and then little flames appeared over each person. The Holy Spirit gave each person the ability to speak different languages. Some people thought the believers were all drunk, but Peter explained what had happened.

Action Adventure from Acts 2:1-8, 13-24, 33-41

On the day of Pentecost all the believers were meeting together in one place. Suddenly, there was a sound from heaven like the roaring of a mighty windstorm. Then, what looked like flames or tongues of fire settled on each of them. Everyone present was filled with the Holy Spirit and began speaking in other languages.

At that time there were devout Jews from every nation living in Jerusalem. When they heard the noise, everyone came running. "How can this be?" they exclaimed. "These people are all from Galilee, and yet we hear them speaking in our own native languages!"

Others ridiculed them, saying, "They're just drunk!"

Then Peter shouted to the crowd, "These people are not drunk. No, what you see was predicted long ago by the prophet Joel: 'In the last days,' God says, 'I will pour out my Spirit upon all people. And I will cause wonders in the heavens above and signs on the earth below. Everyone who calls on the name of the LORD will be saved.'

Key Verse

"In the last days," God says, "I will pour out my Spirit upon all people. Your sons and daughters will prophesy. Your young men will see visions, and your old men will dream dreams."

Acts 2:17

"God endorsed Jesus the Nazarene by doing powerful miracles, wonders, and signs through him. But God knew what would happen, and his plan was carried out when Jesus was betrayed. You nailed him to a cross and killed him. But God released him from the horrors of death and raised him back to life, for death could not keep him in its grip.

"Now he is exalted to the place of highest honor in heaven, at God's right hand. And the Father gave him the Holy Spirit to pour out upon us, just as you see today."

Peter's words pierced their hearts, and they said to him and to the other apostles, "Brothers, what should we do?"

Peter replied, "Repent of your sins and be baptized in the name of Jesus for the forgiveness of your sins. Then you will receive the Holy Spirit." Those who

I knew we were helpers, but this is pretty crazy.

believed what Peter said were baptized and added to the church that day—about 3,000 in all.

The believers devoted themselves to the apostles' teaching, and to fellowship, and to sharing in meals, and to prayer. The believers met together in one place and shared everything they had. And each day the Lord added to their fellowship those who were being saved.

Now What?

The Holy Spirit came to believers and immediately changed their lives. They were able to speak other languages so people from all around the world could understand them. It was amazing. Peter explained that when you are sorry for your sin and turn away from it, you will receive the Holy Spirit. Then your job is to study God's Word, talk with him in prayer, and get to know him better and better. As you do that, the Holy Spirit will teach you how to serve God. And he will help you do the work!

95

A LAME MAN WALKS

What's Up

Peter and John, two of Jesus' followers, were among those who received the Holy Spirit after Jesus went to heaven. One day as they were going into the Temple, a man who couldn't walk stopped them and asked them for money. Peter had something even better to give the man.

Action Adventure from Acts 3

Peter and John went to the Temple one afternoon to take part in the three o'clock prayer service. As they approached the Temple, a man lame from birth was being carried in. Each day he was put beside the Temple gate so he could beg from the people going into the Temple. When he saw Peter and John about to enter, he asked them for some money.

Peter and John looked at him, and Peter said, "Look at us!" The lame man looked at them, expecting some money. But Peter said, "I don't have any silver or gold for you. But I'll give you what I have. In the name of Jesus Christ, get up and walk!"

Then Peter took the man by the hand and helped him up. As he did, the man's feet and ankles were instantly healed. He stood on his feet and began to walk! Then, walking, leaping, and praising God, he went into the Temple with them.

The people saw him walking and heard him praising God. When they realized he was the lame beggar they had seen so often, they rushed out to where the man was holding tightly to Peter and John.

Peter addressed the crowd. "Why stare at us as though we had made this man walk by our own power? It is the God of Abraham, Isaac, and Jacob who brought glory to his servant Jesus by doing this. This is the same Jesus whom you rejected

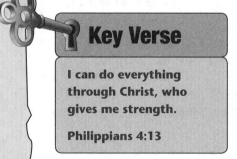

Key Verse

I can do everything through Christ, who gives me strength.

Philippians 4:13

before Pilate. You killed the author of life, but God raised him from the dead. Through faith in Jesus, this man was healed.

"What you did to Jesus was done in ignorance. Now repent and turn to God, so your sins may be wiped away. Then he will again send you Jesus. For he must remain in heaven until the time for the final restoration of all things. Moses said, 'The LORD your God will raise up for you a Prophet from among your own people. Listen carefully to everything he tells you. Anyone who will not listen to that Prophet will be completely cut off from God's people.'

"Every prophet spoke about what is happening today. You are the children of those prophets, and you are included

I'll take this over a few coins any day!

in the covenant God promised to your ancestors. For God said to Abraham, 'Through your descendants all the families on earth will be blessed.' When God raised up his servant, Jesus, he sent him first to you, to bless you by turning each of you back from your sinful ways."

Now What?

It must have felt amazing for Peter to be able to heal a lame man. But Peter knew (and told everyone) that the power didn't come from him— the power came from God. That power is ready for everyone who loves God to use. There is no end to the things you can do. When you have work to do for God or when you have a problem that you must face, God's power will give you the strength to do it!

96

THE MEETING ON THE DAMASCUS ROAD

What's Up

Saul did not like Christians. He persecuted them. That means he harassed them. He did it by arresting them and making their lives miserable. Saul got an okay to go to the city of Damascus and arrest the Christians there. But on the way there, a bright light shone down on him and Jesus spoke to him. Right there on the road to Damascus, Saul met Jesus!

Action Adventure from Acts 9:1-20

Saul was uttering threats with every breath and was eager to kill the Lord's followers. So he went to the high priest. He requested letters to the synagogues in Damascus, asking for their cooperation in the arrest of any followers he found there. He wanted to bring both men and women back to Jerusalem in chains.

As he was approaching Damascus, a light from heaven suddenly shone down around him. He fell to the ground and heard a voice saying, "Saul! Saul! Why are you persecuting me?"

"Who are you, lord?" Saul asked.

The voice replied, "I am Jesus, the one you are persecuting! Get up and go into the city, and you will be told what you must do."

The men with Saul heard the sound of someone's voice but saw no one! Saul picked himself up, but when he opened his eyes he was blind. So his companions led him by the hand to Damascus. He remained blind for three days and did not eat or drink.

Now there was a believer in Damascus named Ananias. The Lord spoke to him in a vision, calling, "Ananias!"

"Yes, Lord!" he replied.

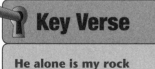

Key Verse

He alone is my rock and my salvation, my fortress where I will not be shaken.

Psalm 62:6

The Lord said, "Go over to Straight Street, to the house of Judas. Ask for a man from Tarsus named Saul. He is praying to me right now. I have shown him a vision of a man named Ananias coming in and laying hands on him so he can see again."

"But Lord," exclaimed Ananias, "I've heard about the terrible things this man has done to the believers in Jerusalem! And he is authorized by the leading priests to arrest everyone who calls upon your name."

But the Lord said, "Saul is to take my message to the Gentiles and to kings, as well as to the people of Israel. I will show him how much he must suffer for my name's sake."

So Ananias went and found Saul. He laid his hands on him and said, "Brother Saul, the Lord Jesus, who appeared to you on the road, has sent me so that

Wow! He can really get someone's attention!

you might regain your sight and be filled with the Holy Spirit." Instantly something like scales fell from Saul's eyes, and he regained his sight. Then he got up and was baptized. Afterward he ate some food and regained his strength. Immediately he began preaching about Jesus in the synagogues, saying, "He is indeed the Son of God!"

Now What?

Saul was excited about attacking Christians. After he met Jesus, he became excited about telling others about Jesus. Saul was saved from living a life of sin, and he became a new person.

He changed his name to Paul and spent the rest of his life teaching and speaking about Jesus. When you met Jesus, did you choose to believe in him? If so, how did it change your life? Are your habits different? Do you spend your time in different ways? Is it important to you to tell others about Jesus? Do people around you know that you belong to him?

97

THE TROUBLE WITH GENTILES

What's Up

Cornelius was a Gentile—a person who is not Jewish. When an angel visited Cornelius in a vision, he was afraid. The angel knew that Cornelius feared God, so he told him to send for Peter. At the same time, Peter had a vision. It was like they were having a dream while they were awake. God told Peter it was okay to talk with Gentiles.

Action Adventure from Acts 10

A Roman army officer named Cornelius gave to the poor and prayed to God. One afternoon, he had a vision in which he saw an angel of God coming toward him. "Cornelius!" the angel said.

"What is it, sir?" [Cornelius] asked.

The angel replied, "Your prayers and gifts to the poor have been received by God as an offering! Send some men to Joppa and summon Peter."

Cornelius sent [three men] off to Joppa.

The next day, Peter went up on the roof to pray. It was about noon, and he was hungry. While a meal was being prepared, he fell into a trance. He saw the sky open, and a large sheet was let down by its four corners. In the sheet were all sorts of animals, reptiles, and birds. Then a voice said, "Kill and eat them."

"No, Lord," Peter declared. "I have never eaten anything that our Jewish laws have declared impure and unclean."

But the voice spoke again: "Do not call something unclean if God has made it clean."

As Peter was puzzling over the vision, the Holy Spirit said, "Three men have come looking for you. Go with them. I have sent them."

Key Verse

He is the one all the prophets testified about, saying that everyone who believes in him will have their sins forgiven through his name.

Acts 10:43

So Peter went down and said, "I'm the man you are looking for. Why have you come?"

They said, "We were sent by Cornelius, a Roman officer. An angel instructed him to summon you to his house so that he can hear your message." The next day [Peter] went with them.

Cornelius had called together his relatives and close friends. Peter told them, "It is against our laws for a Jewish man to enter a Gentile home. But God has shown me that I should no longer think of anyone as impure or unclean. Tell me why you sent for me."

Cornelius replied, "We are waiting to hear the message the Lord has given you."

Peter replied, "This is the message of Good News—there is peace with God through Jesus Christ. God anointed Jesus with the Holy Spirit and with power. Then Jesus went around healing all who were oppressed by the devil, for God was with him.

This is going to get really interesting!

"They put him to death, but God raised him to life on the third day. He is the one all the prophets testified about, saying that everyone who believes in him will have their sins forgiven through his name."

Even as Peter was saying these things, the Holy Spirit fell upon all who were listening. So he gave orders for them to be baptized in the name of Jesus Christ.

Now What?

There are many different churches today, and they often think their way is the only right way. That was true even in Peter's time as Jews and Gentiles wouldn't worship together. What was the point of Peter's vision? That anyone who follows Jesus should get along with anyone else who follows Jesus. They should all show love and kindness toward one another and toward those who do not yet know God.

98

SINGING IN JAIL

What's Up

Paul and Silas prayed until a demon left a slave girl. Then she could no longer tell fortunes. Her owners got mad and had Paul and Silas put in jail. They were chained and their feet were placed in stocks—wooden frames with holes to put feet through and lock. As Paul and Silas were singing praises to God, an earthquake shook the prison, breaking open the doors and setting the prisoners free. But then Paul did something surprising!

Action Adventure from Acts 16:16-40

A demon-possessed slave girl was a fortune-teller who earned a lot of money for her masters. She followed Paul and [his friends], shouting, "These men are servants of the Most High God, and they have come to tell you how to be saved."

This went on day after day until Paul said to the demon within her, "I command you in the name of Jesus Christ to come out of her." And instantly it left her.

Her masters' hopes of wealth were now shattered, so they grabbed Paul and Silas and dragged them before the authorities. "The whole city is in an uproar because of these Jews!" they shouted to the city officials. "They are teaching customs that are illegal."

Paul and Silas were beaten and thrown into prison. The jailer put them in the inner dungeon and clamped their feet in stocks.

Around midnight Paul and Silas were praying and singing hymns to God, and the other prisoners were listening. Suddenly, there was an earthquake. All the doors flew open and the chains of every prisoner fell off! The jailer woke up to see the prison doors open. He assumed the prisoners had escaped, so he drew his sword to kill himself. But Paul shouted, "Stop! We are all here!"

Key Verse

Believe in the Lord Jesus and you will be saved, along with everyone in your household.

Acts 16:31

The jailer ran to the dungeon and fell down before Paul and Silas and asked, "Sirs, what must I do to be saved?"

They replied, "Believe in the Lord Jesus and you will be saved, along with everyone in your household." They shared the word of the Lord with him and all who lived in his household. The jailer cared for them and washed their wounds. Then he and everyone in his household were baptized. He brought them into his house and set a meal before them, and his entire household rejoiced because they all believed in God.

The next morning the city officials sent the police to tell the jailer, "Let those men go!"

So the jailer told Paul, "The city officials have said you and Silas are free to leave. Go in peace."

But Paul replied, "They have beaten us without a trial and put us in prison—and we are Roman

He's not going to believe this!

citizens. Now they want us to leave secretly? Certainly not! Let them come to release us!"

The city officials were alarmed to learn that Paul and Silas were Roman citizens. So they came to the jail and apologized to them. Then they begged them to leave the city. When Paul and Silas left the prison, they met with the believers and encouraged them once more. Then they left town.

Now What?

Even in prison, Paul and Silas sang praises to God. They didn't feel down or sad about being in prison. They weren't afraid. They trusted God, and they showed their faith in God by praising him and by not trying to escape. Their faith led the jailer and his whole family to trust Jesus! You never know when someone else will notice your trust in God and will learn to trust him too! It's especially likely to happen if you trust God during a difficult time.

99

SHIPWRECKED!

What's Up

Some of the Jewish leaders in Jerusalem didn't like Paul's preaching. To keep him safe, Roman soldiers arrested him and put him on a ship sailing for Rome. There he would be put on trial. However, as the ship sailed, the weather turned bad and the sailors were afraid that they would be shipwrecked. God told Paul that the ship would be wrecked but no one on the ship would die.

Action Adventure from Acts 27:1, 7-14, 18-44

We set sail for Italy. Paul and several other prisoners were placed in the custody of a Roman officer. We had several days of slow sailing. The weather was becoming dangerous for sea travel because it was so late in the fall, and Paul spoke to the ship's officers about it.

"Men," he said, "I believe there is trouble if we go on—shipwreck, loss of cargo, and danger to our lives as well." But the officer in charge of the prisoners listened more to the ship's captain than to Paul.

When wind began blowing from the south, the sailors thought they could make it. But the weather changed, and a wind of typhoon strength blew us out to sea.

The next day, as gale-force winds continued to batter the ship, the crew began throwing the cargo overboard. The terrible storm raged for many days until all hope was gone. Paul called the crew together and said, "None of you will lose your lives, even though the ship will go down. Last night an angel of God said, 'God in his goodness has granted safety to everyone sailing with you.' I believe God. But we will be shipwrecked on an island."

About midnight on the fourteenth night of the storm,

Key Verse

I trust in your unfailing love. I will rejoice because you have rescued me.

Psalm 13:5

the sailors tried to abandon the ship. But Paul said to the commanding officer and the soldiers, "You will all die unless the sailors stay aboard." So the soldiers cut the ropes to the lifeboat and let it drift away.

As day was dawning, Paul urged everyone to eat. "You haven't touched food for two weeks," he said. "Eat now for your own good. For not a hair of your heads will perish." Then he took some bread, gave thanks to God before them all, and broke off a piece and ate it. Then everyone was encouraged and began to eat.

When morning dawned, they wondered if they could get to shore by running the ship aground. So they cut off the anchors and left them in the sea and headed toward shore. But they ran the ship aground too soon. The bow of the ship stuck fast, while the stern was

I know his God can do anything, but that was a little dramatic.

repeatedly smashed by the waves and began to break apart.

The soldiers wanted to kill the prisoners to make sure they didn't escape. But the commanding officer wanted to spare Paul. He ordered all who could swim to jump overboard and make for land. The others held on to planks from the broken ship. So everyone escaped safely to shore.

Now What?

Paul trusted God and stayed in close touch with him through prayer. So it wasn't surprising that God gave him the message about being safe even in a shipwreck. Staying close to God is how you get to know him better. Then you can recognize when he guides you and gives you direction. Trusting God no matter what is happening in your life shows that your trust is real and that you believe he has good plans for you.

100

THE FINAL BATTLE

What's Up

The book of Revelation is God's story of what will happen when Jesus comes back. God told the story to John in a vision—a dream while he was awake. John saw Jesus fighting against Satan, also called the devil. Jesus will win, and then his praises will be heard throughout the whole world. There will be a wedding celebration. The groom will be Jesus, the Lamb of God. The bride will be the church—all the people who love Jesus and follow him. The devil will be tossed into a lake of fire and be punished for eternity—forever and ever.

Action Adventure from Revelation 19

I heard what sounded like a crowd in heaven shouting, "Praise the LORD! Salvation and glory and power belong to our God. His judgments are true and just."

And again their voices rang out: "Praise the LORD!" Then the twenty-four elders and the four living beings fell down and worshiped God, who was sitting on the throne.

Then I heard again the shout of a crowd: "Praise the LORD! Let us rejoice and give honor to him. The time has come for the wedding feast of the Lamb, and his bride has prepared herself. She has been given the finest of pure white linen to wear." The fine linen represents the good deeds of God's holy people.

The angel said, "Blessed are those who are invited to the wedding feast of the Lamb." I fell down at his feet to worship him, but he said, "No, don't worship me. I am a servant of God, just like you and your brothers and sisters who testify about their faith in Jesus. Worship only God. Give a clear witness for Jesus."

I saw heaven opened, and a

Key Verse

Praise the LORD! Salvation and glory and power belong to our God.

Revelation 19:1

white horse was standing there. Its rider was named Faithful and True. His eyes were like flames of fire, and on his head were many crowns. He wore a robe dipped in blood, and his title was the Word of God. The armies of heaven, dressed in the finest of pure white linen, followed him on white horses. He will rule with an iron rod. On his robe was written this title: King of all kings and Lord of all lords.

I can see people arguing about this for hundreds of years!

Then I saw the beast and the kings of the world and their armies gathered to fight the one sitting on the horse and his army. And the beast was captured, and with him the false prophet who did mighty miracles on behalf of the beast—miracles that deceived all who had accepted the mark of the beast. Both the beast and his false prophet were thrown alive into the fiery lake of burning sulfur. Their entire army was killed by the sharp sword that came from the mouth of the one riding the white horse.

Now What?

The battle between good and evil—God and Satan—will happen at the end of time. There is no doubt that God will win. After that battle God and his children will celebrate, but Satan and his followers will not. They will spend eternity being punished. Some people say, "Oh, I will decide to follow God later, when I'm older." But they don't know when the opportunities will run out—when Christ will return and everything will change. Don't wait. Choose Christ today!

101

OUR HOME IN HEAVEN

What's Up

Another part of John's vision was the new Jerusalem—the holy city coming down out of heaven. This is where believers will live forever with Jesus. God will be with his people and there will be no more sadness. There will only be joy as God's people worship him. It will be a beautiful city, decorated with shiny jewels, gold, and silver. But nothing will be more beautiful or wonderful than God himself!

Action Adventure from Revelation 21; 22:1-2, 16, 20-21

I saw a new heaven and a new earth. And I saw the holy city, the new Jerusalem, coming down from God like a bride beautifully dressed for her husband. I heard a loud shout from the throne, saying, "God's home is now among his people! He will live with them, and they will be his people. He will wipe every tear from their eyes, and there will be no more death or sorrow or crying or pain."

The one on the throne said, "I am the Alpha and Omega—the Beginning and End. To all who are thirsty I will be their God, and they will be my children. But unbelievers, murderers, the immoral, those who practice witchcraft, idol worshipers, and liars—their fate is in the fiery lake."

One of the seven angels said, "I will show you the bride." The holy city, Jerusalem, [descended] from God. It shone with the glory of God and sparkled like a precious stone. The city wall was broad and high, with twelve gates guarded by angels. The names of the twelve tribes of Israel were written on the gates. The wall had twelve foundation stones,

Key Verse

He will wipe every tear from their eyes, and there will be no more death or sorrow or crying or pain. All these things are gone forever.

Revelation 21:4

and on them were written the names of the twelve apostles.

The angel held a gold measuring stick. When he measured [the city], he found it was a square.

The city was pure gold. The twelve gates were pearls—each gate a single pearl! The main street was pure gold, as clear as glass.

The city has no need of sun or moon, for the glory of God and the Lamb is its light. There is no night there. Nothing evil will be allowed to enter—only those whose names are written in the Lamb's Book of Life.

The angel showed me a river with the water of life flowing from the throne of God. On each side of the river grew a tree of life, bearing twelve crops

It looks every bit as good as promised!

of fruit, with a fresh crop each month. The leaves were used for medicine to heal the nations.

"I, Jesus, have sent my angel to give you this message for the churches. I am coming soon!"

Amen! Come, Lord Jesus! May the grace of the Lord Jesus be with God's holy people.

Now What?

God promises that one day Jesus will return and that all believers will live with him forever. That's the reason Jesus died for our sins . . . so that we could be pure and ready to be in God's holy presence. Do hearing and reading about heaven make you eager for Jesus to come back? As you wait, praise him. And love him today!